Developing Adolescent Literacy in the Online Classroom

Developing Adolescent Literacy in the Online Classroom

Strategies for All Content Areas

Brooke Eisenbach
Paula Greathouse

ROWMAN & LITTLEFIELD
Lanham • Boulder • New York • London

Published by Rowman & Littlefield
An imprint of The Rowman & Littlefield Publishing Group, Inc.
4501 Forbes Boulevard, Suite 200, Lanham, Maryland 20706
www.rowman.com

6 Tinworth Street, London SE11 5AL, United Kingdom

Copyright © 2020 by Brooke Eisenbach and Paula Greathouse

All rights reserved. No part of this book may be reproduced in any form or by any electronic or mechanical means, including information storage and retrieval systems, without written permission from the publisher, except by a reviewer who may quote passages in a review.

British Library Cataloguing in Publication Information Available

Library of Congress Cataloging-in-Publication Data

Names: Eisenbach, Brooke, author. | Greathouse, Paula, author.
Title: Developing adolescent literacy in the online classroom : strategies for all content areas / Brooke Eisenbach, Paula Greathouse.
Description: Lanham : Rowman & Littlefield, [2020] | Includes bibliographical references. | Summary: "This book provides middle and high school virtual teachers a variety of strategies for translating traditional literacy instructional practices from the brick-and-mortar classroom to the online learning context."—Provided by publisher.
Identifiers: LCCN 2020004789 (print) | LCCN 2020004790 (ebook) | ISBN 9781475851014 (cloth) | ISBN 9781475851021 (paperback) | ISBN 9781475851038 (epub)
Subjects: LCSH: Language arts (Middle school)—Computer-assisted instruction. | Language arts (Secondary)—Computer-assisted instruction. | Literacy. | Web-based instruction. | Computers and literacy.
Classification: LCC LB1631.3 .E37 2020 (print) | LCC LB1631.3 (ebook) | DDC 428.0071/20285—dc23
LC record available at https://lccn.loc.gov/2020004789
LC ebook record available at https://lccn.loc.gov/2020004790

Contents

Introduction ... vii

1 Setting the Foundation for a Successful Course: Strategies for Building Relationships and Community ... 1
2 Motivating Readers and Writers in the Online Classroom ... 13
3 Uncovering Reading and Writing Identities ... 23
4 Getting Ready to Read and Write ... 29
5 Questioning ... 39
6 Online Classroom Conversation and Collaboration ... 45
7 Engaging Critical Literacies in the Online Classroom ... 57
8 Assessing Reading Comprehension ... 69
9 Engaging in the Writing Process ... 77
10 Engaging Online Students in Multiple Forms of Writing ... 87
11 Conducting Writing Assessments in the Online Classroom ... 99

References ... 105
About the Authors ... 109

Introduction

If anyone suggested that we would one day teach students in a virtual capacity—in a "classroom" separated by both time and space—we would have assumed they were speaking of a world only found within the pages of a science fiction novel. Online teaching and learning? What is that? How does that work? How do we effectively teach students we never meet?

Our education programs in college prepared us for classroom teaching. Our professors helped guide us in understanding adolescent development, pedagogy, and classroom content. As we entered the profession, we gained experience working with our students. With each passing year, we uncovered ways of connecting, building community, and guiding learners as readers and writers. Our methods relied on the traditional setting. How could such strategies and experiences translate to this new learning context?

Designing and implementing effective literacy instructional approaches for students can be one of the most pressing challenges facing schools, including virtual schools. Neglecting to consider the magnitude of literacy skills needed in today's world, and not teaching literacy effectively, may lead to difficulties later in life (Costa & Kallick, 2000; Houge et al., 2007). Despite the growing population of learners attending school in the online space, many of today's virtual teachers lack formal preparation for virtual literacy instruction. For most educators, their toolbox of literacy strategies focuses on approaches intended for the traditional classroom context. But methods of reading and writing within the online classroom differ from that of the brick-and-mortar environment. Instead of engaging with one another in a face-to-face setting, virtual students are educated through synchronous and asynchronous channels. Often separated by time and space, virtual teachers encounter a greater degree of difficulty in connecting, engaging, and communicating with students (Eisenbach et al., 2018). Thankfully, research in virtual education points to the growth and development of new, inclusive virtual means of fostering student literacy growth. Adolescent readers and writers can utilize new technologies, and teachers can implement a diverse array of instructional strategies in the reading, discussion, analysis, and writing of texts.

As a growing body of diverse adolescent learners sign into virtual classrooms, it is essential that online educators uncover effective tools and strategies for developing literacy and engaging online learners in literacy practices. Additionally, twenty-first-century task demands require students to become literate beyond content. As virtual educators, it becomes imperative to include pedagogical approaches that allow adolescent learners to read, write, and discuss both the word and the world in an effort to promote equity, access, and opportunity. But what do these strategies look like in the virtual classroom?

In recent years, we have had the honor of meeting and chatting with teachers from across the country. Our conversations with virtual teachers pointed toward a need for strategies that encourage the literacy development of online learners. The goal of this text is to provide teachers a starting point in considering how we might effectively transfer our knowledge of literacy pedagogy to the online learning platform. In other words, we want virtual teachers, or teachers who are teaching in hybrid courses or wish to include technology in the classroom, to utilize this book as a guide to taking traditional literacy strategies learned in their teacher preparation and transfer these to the virtual environment.

BOOK ORGANIZATION

Before focusing on the academic, we must find ways to cultivate community with virtual learners. In the early chapters, we focus on setting the stage for effective virtual learning. We begin by sharing strategies for establishing and maintaining effective communication with students and families (chapter 1). We then move forward in sharing techniques for motivating online learners towards consistent, active engagement in the virtual setting (chapter 2). Finally, we offer strategies intended to aid online learners in forging their unique reader and writer identities (chapter 3).

We then transition from establishing connections to sharing strategies for encouraging and educating our virtual students as literacy learners—assisting virtual learners getting ready to read and write (chapter 4), formulating questions during the reading process (chapter 5), collaborating and conversing with fellow virtual learners (chapter 6), and engaging in critical literacy (chapter 7). This portion of the book highlights pedagogy that translates to the virtual classroom as we assist our students in growing as critical consumers of knowledge. After sharing strategies for reading development, we conclude with suggestions for virtual reading comprehension assessment (chapter 8).

The final chapters move from the focus on reading to a focus on writing. We begin by providing virtual teachers insight into instruction and applications that aid online learners throughout the writing process—from brainstorming to outlining to drafting and finalizing text (chapter 9). Then, we offer techniques for engaging virtual learners in multiple forms and purposes of writing (chapter 10). Finally, we round out the section with attention to writing assessment and accountability within the online context (chapter 11).

As teachers, we know what works for our students. But we might struggle in navigating this new context and transitioning our best practices to a new, ever-expanding space. Our goal with this book is to provide a starting point for online teachers as they seek out ways to translate effective literacy pedagogy from the traditional classroom to the virtual platform. As you engage with these chapters, we hope our work can assist you in moving an eye toward the future of education, and in meeting the needs of our adolescent learners within this new setting.

Note to Readers: As you read this book, please note that the terms *online* and *virtual* are used synonymously.

Chapter One

Setting the Foundation for a Successful Course

Strategies for Building Relationships and Community

If we were to ask you to take a moment and recall a teacher who made a positive, lasting impression in your life, it's likely you will reflect on an educator who cared about you in some unique way. Perhaps you'll consider a teacher who shared a passion for a particular subject or content—someone who nurtured a love of learning. Or, maybe you will remember a teacher who took time to listen and foster a relationship with you—an individual who helped you through a trying time in your life. Regardless of our unique experiences, it's easy to agree that teachers who demonstrate care and strive to cultivate positive relationships within the classroom are in a position to encourage adolescent learning and development.

Teaching is a profession that entails both instructional and relational responsibilities. While academic knowledge and skills are important, caring relationships are foundational to a strong educational environment (Lake et al., 2014; Owusu-Ansah & Kyei-Blankson, 2016). As we transition away from the traditional school context and focus our attention on the virtual space, it's important to remember that relationships and community are still essential to our students' cognitive, social, and emotional growth. A lack of relationships impedes our ability as educators to motivate, engage, and connect our students with the academic goals of our online classroom and curriculum.

Relationships within a classroom directly influence a learning community's literacy practices (Bloome, 2001). As virtual teachers strive to connect with online learners, and in turn identify ways to connect students within the classroom community, it is important to remember that care and community are essential to shaping the discourses vital to engaging in critical literacy (Thomas et al., 2015; White, 2003). And while we understand the importance of fostering a classroom through connection and care, the question becomes one of transitioning such relationships to the online platform. How can we, as virtual teachers, open the door to positive relationships outside of the traditional classroom space? How might we get to know our students—their interests, needs, strengths, cultures, and more—and utilize this knowledge to set a foundation for connection that transcends space and time? How might we promote the collective caring of the online classroom community without the benefit of immediacy and face-to-face engagement?

Through a variety of strategies, virtual teachers can foster positive relationships with online learners and provide opportunities for students to connect and get to know one another. The intention here is to introduce a space for virtual teachers and learners to "meet" and connect, knowing that relationships take consistent time, effort, and reflection. The strategies we offer help to provide an essential platform from which online classroom communities can continue to grow and flourish throughout the literacy learning process.

STRATEGIES FOR INTRODUCING RELATIONSHIPS AND COMMUNITY IN THE VIRTUAL CLASSROOM

Interest Inventories

While the general idea of an interest inventory is nothing new to the classroom, the significance of such an inventory to opening dialogue within the online space cannot be overstated. The online learning environment has the potential to be a place of isolation. In an effort to combat this lack of connection, it is important to begin by asking questions and invest in student interests. An interest inventory provides teachers and students insights into one another's interests, thereby offering a terrific starting point for identifying individual similarities and unique differences, engaging in low-risk conversation, and providing insights into potential topics for curriculum and student choice.

Interest inventories, sometimes referred to as interest surveys, are questionnaires that ask students to share or rate their enjoyment and interest in a wide variety of activities and topics. The inventories can be content specific (see figures 1.1 and 1.2), or general in nature. Below are sample questions or prompts that a teacher can include in a general interest inventory:

- Provide three adjectives that describe you.

- What type of music do you listen to? Who is your favorite musician or band?
- What was the last movie you watched? What is your favorite movie?
- What is your favorite TV show?
- What do you like to do in your spare time (evenings, weekends)?
- What sports do you like to play, if any?
- If you could go on a trip anywhere in the world, where would it be?
- If you could go back in time, where would you go and why?
- Do you have any pets? If so, what kind, and what are their names?
- Do you like to create art (paintings, sculpture, music, etc.)? If so, what type?
- Do you take any types of lessons (dance, music, etc.)? If so, what type?
- Do you have a part-time job? If so, where?
- If you had a million dollars, what would you spend it on?

While very easy to craft, there are a plethora of readily available interest inventories that virtual teachers can use or adapt to meet their purpose.

Just like there are many interest inventory formats, there are also many ways a virtual teacher can approach an interest inventory in the online space. Virtual teachers can send students an interest inventory as an email attachment, asking students to complete and send back. Or a virtual teacher can create a video with a list of questions and ask students to respond via VoiceThread or through the creation of a Flipgrid video to be shared with their classmates. But no matter the format in survey or approach, what is most important is virtual teachers getting to know their students on a personal level, and students getting to know each other as a means of creating a community of care in the online space.

Creating a Course Avatar

A creative and fun alternative to sharing a photo is the creation of an original course avatar. Students can share aspects of their identity, experience, and interests through the original composition of a unique avatar they can utilize throughout their time in the course. What might they dream up? Who might they be?

There are a wide array of free online resources designed for the creation of such avatars, such as Voki, Kartunix, Avatar Maker, Avachara, and DoppleMe. Virtual teachers can share such resources with virtual learners following course enrollment. Students can select the resource that works for them, based on their current level of technological knowledge and literacy. Once they create their unique avatar, students can share their work with their classmates, as well as with the course instructor. Virtual instructors are encouraged to create a course avatar, as well.

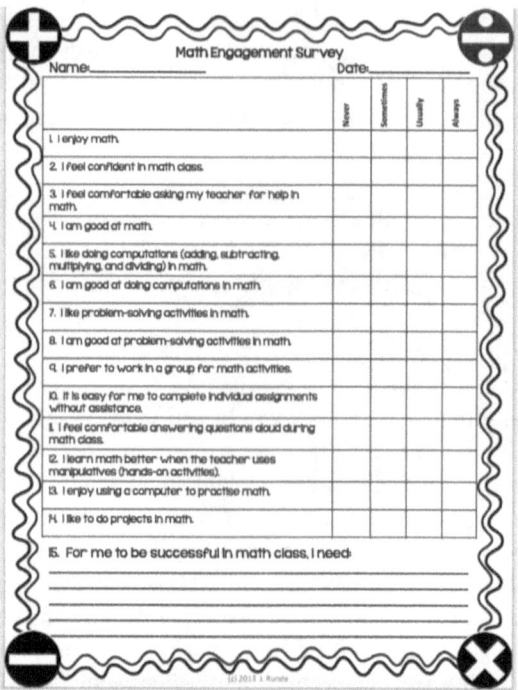

Figure 1.1. Sample Math Engagement Survey, created by J. Runde. *Courtesy of TPT*

Phone Calls/Video Chats

There is power in human connection. And, while online platforms vary in their nature and structure, nothing promotes such connection as strongly as the immediacy of a phone call or video chat. Phone calls and video chats put a voice and a face to the name on the other side of the computer screen. They bring a much-needed element of humanity to our technological space. Yet, even something as seemingly simplistic as a phone call can pose a challenge for virtual teachers and learners. In the traditional classroom we can greet our students, face to face, as they walk through the door. Eye contact, facial expressions, body language, and proximity allow us to engage in conversation, exchange a smile, or respond to a moment of confusion or need. This is not the case when it comes to the asynchronous nature of online learning. For this reason, it is even more imperative that virtual teachers take the initiative to establish two-way communication with learners through synchronous means.

```
                                        Name: _____
                    Science Interest Survey
        Put a checkmark next to the things you like to do during science class.
        ___ watch science movies / videos
        ___ read about science in a magazine / book
        ___ do research about science on the computer
        ___ create and build models of real-life things
        ___ do science experiments alone
        ___ do science experiments with partners


        Circle 5 things you are most interested in learning more about.
        weather          space           rockets         rocks and minerals
        roller coasters  computers       robots          animals
        states of matter force and motion chemistry      plants


        My favorite thing about science is ...
        _____
        _____

        One question I have about science is...
        _____
        _____

        What are your hobbies or favorite activities to do at home?
        _____
        _____

        If you could be anything in the world when you grow up, what would you be? Why?
        _____
        _____

        If you were given $1,000, what would you do with it?
        _____
        _____
```

Figure 1.2. Sample Science Interest Survey, created by Coleman's Creative Classroom. *Courtesy of TPT*

Introductory phone calls or video chats allow virtual educators an opportunity to "meet" students and initiate dialogue with families. While it is important to take time during the call to introduce learners and guardians to the online classroom technology, curriculum, and course expectations, it is also vital that we ask questions and seek out information regarding each student's background, experience, interests, needs, and more. Engage learners in a personable discussion—one that serves as a foundation for connections you can draw upon and build from for the duration of the course.

In addition, teachers should use the initial call to establish preferred methods and times for future contact. It can be challenging to connect with learners throughout the academic year. Separation of time and space often limit a teacher's or a student's ability to establish contact in moments of academic need. By opening lines of communication early, both parties are more likely to establish a timeframe and method of contact that works for everyone involved.

STRATEGIES FOR GETTING TO KNOW YOUR STUDENTS AS READERS AND WRITERS

Reading and Writing Survey

With literacy at the center of all content areas, it is important that virtual teachers get to know their students as readers and writers. Janet Allen (2000) reminds us that "In schools where educators have listened to students' voices and developed instructional practices that helped overcome barriers to literacy success, great improvements in students' literacy have been made" (pp. 59–60). One way that virtual teachers can solicit student voices and perspectives on reading and writing is through reading and writing surveys.

There are several free reading and writing surveys available for teachers to use. Some surveys solely focus on reading, some on writing, and some combine the two. Because reading and writing are linked, we suggest utilizing a survey that tackles both topics (see figure 1.3). Additionally, if creating your own survey, we suggest that questions and prompts on reading and writing are both given equal weight.

In developing adolescent literacy in online spaces, it is also important to discover the literacy practices our students participate in outside the classroom. As such, we suggest that you include an opportunity for students to share with you the types of reading they do and the genres and formats that interest them the most. For example, virtual teachers can give their students a list and ask them to check off the types of texts they enjoy reading: mysteries, adventure stories, biographies, autobiographies, folktales, fantasy, poetry, and so on. They can also provide students with a list of text formats and have them share which ones they enjoy reading the most: graphic novels, series texts, chapter books, magazines, picture books, digital texts, and so on. The same can be done with writing.

With any survey, there are multiple options for teachers to administer and collect responses. Virtual teachers can opt to have their students complete a reading and writing survey in a Word document format, through a survey site such as SurveyMonkey, or through the creation of video responses.

READING-WRITING SURVEY

- What does one have to do in order to be a good writer?
- What is the easiest part of writing for you? What do you do well?
- What is the hardest part of writing for you? What do you need to work on?
- How do you come up with ideas for writing?
- What are the qualities of good writing?
- What is the best piece of writing you've ever done? What made it so good?
- What helps you the most to make your writing better?
- What kind of response helps you the most as a writer? Who gives you that response?
- Why is it important to be able to write well?
- What do you like about writing?
- What happens to your finished pieces of writing?
- How did you learn to write?
- What kind of writing do you do *just for you*?
- What does one have to do in order to be a good reader?
- What makes reading easy for you?
- How do you go about choosing books to read?
- What are the qualities you look for in a good book?
- What's the best book you've ever read? What made it so good?
- How did you learn to read?
- What kind of reading do you do *just for you*?
- What do you think are the connections between reading and writing?
- How does the ability to do one, help you with the other?

Figure 1.3. Sample Reading and Writing Survey (included in Linda Rief's book, *Seeking Diversity*, pp. 270–271). *Adapted from Nancie Atwell's book,* In the Middle, *available at studylib.net*

Book Talks

Book talks are a common method of book sharing and book swapping within the traditional classroom space. Teachers and students share out summaries and key points of familiar and favorite titles as a means of encouraging others to read selected works. Teachers can introduce new titles through creative book introductions as a way of enticing students to pick up a copy of the book and begin reading. This common strategy can be carried over to the online classroom as a means of learning more about the reading tendencies and preferences of online learners. What books do online learners enjoy reading? Who are their favorite authors? What genres do they commonly encounter?

Rather than engage in a face-to-face book talk, virtual teachers can utilize a variety of online applications and websites to encourage student sharing. Applications like Flipgrid (see figure 1.4) and VoiceThread can provide students a way to video record their book talks, exchange and share their book talks with the teacher and fellow students, and also link potential readers to online resources such as book reviews, author information, or local library websites. Online resources can also provide space for students to comment on and respond to the book talks shared by their peers, thereby encouraging collaboration, questions, and dialogue surrounding selected book titles.

STRATEGIES FOR STUDENTS GETTING TO KNOW EACH OTHER

Photograph Introductions

Photograph introductions can be so much more than the exchange of selfies or portraits. Virtual teachers can utilize photograph introductions in a multitude of ways as a method for allowing students to meet one another within an asynchronous environment. One way of engaging in this strategy is to have

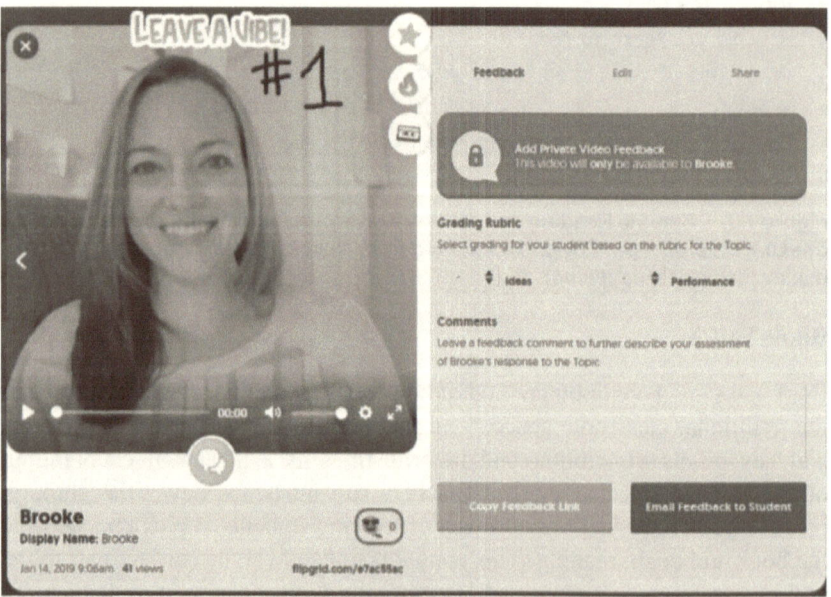

Figure 1.4. Flipgrid screenshot. *Courtesy of the authors*

students share a self-photo, along with a written description of their personal identity, experiences, and interests. The teacher can compile student submissions into a class collage, or a class information sheet to share out with students.

However, teachers can take things a step further and provide students opportunities to get creative in sharing more about themselves with classmates. Rather than rely only on self-portraits, students can illustrate, share images, or craft a unique collage of their life, experiences, or metaphorical representations of their life. Perhaps students view themselves as avid athletes. These students might be encouraged to craft a collage of images depicting their experiences with sports. Or, perhaps they enjoy reading and writing poetry. In this case, students might enjoy sharing this passion through images that symbolically represent their love of words and story.

No matter the method or choice of image, teachers can implement this activity as a means of learning more about the students, and promoting a sense of connection and community within the online classroom space.

Peer Interviews

It's one thing for the teacher to survey and learn more about student experiences outside of the classroom setting. It is another thing for students to take on more of a leadership role in the process of uncovering the experiences, strengths, and interests of their classmates. Traditional classrooms provide ample space and time for students to connect, collaborate, and forge friendships in face-to-face encounters. Students engage with one another in both academic and social settings throughout the school and community space. However, as online classrooms have the potential to isolate learners, this can severely limit peer-to-peer interaction and connection.

Peer interviews offer online learners the opportunity to interact, learn from, and connect with classmates. Students ask questions, share anecdotes, discover similarities, as well as celebrate their unique identities. There are a variety of ways in which a virtual teacher might approach this strategy within the online classroom. Depending on the teacher's location, the nature of the online course and structure, student demographics, and student location, the virtual educator will make judgements regarding how best to connect learners to encourage initial and ongoing peer-to-peer communication. For instance, some students might be able to connect within a synchronous platform to communicate and share information with one another. In the event that a synchronous session is not feasible, virtual teachers can adapt the strategy through the use of a variety of online video or asynchronous communication platforms, then provide students access to the technology and work with learners on interview protocol, time expectations, and expectations for sharing information among classmates.

Regardless of the selected platform or approach, the key is to provide students a safe space in which to encounter, ask questions, and establish connections with their classmates. It's important for online learners to fully realize they are not alone within their course engagement. Peers are an essential piece to the development of our adolescent learners. Student-to-student interviews provide an initial contact to what might develop into social connections and collaboration.

Student of the Week

Rather than drawing on "student of the week" as a means of extrinsic reward for student progress or achievement, virtual teachers can utilize this strategy as a way of learning more about individual students, and sharing that knowledge with the class. For this activity, simply select a different student to highlight on the course page, or in a class newsletter each week. Connect with the selected student via phone or online conferencing channels, and ask questions that provide you insight into the student's interests, hobbies, culture, family, and life outside of the classroom. How do they spend time outside of class? What are some of their favorite family traditions? What are their personal hobbies and interests?

As you engage in conversation with the student, don't be afraid to disclose a little about yourself in the process. This is not only a chance to learn more about the individual student, but it also serves as opportunity to connect and allow the student to see that you are more than a name behind the computer screen. While you want to ensure that the information you choose to share is appropriate to the student-teacher relationship, it is important that you provide your students the opportunity to know more about you, thereby eroding the dissonance that might otherwise pervade the online space.

As you learn more about the student, be sure you are transparent in your intentions. Let them know you would like to share a bit about them with the class, and that you would like to highlight them as the student of the week. Be certain the student is comfortable with your intentions and approves of the information you intend to share out to the online community. We also suggest informing the student's family or guardians of your intentions, especially if you intend to share the student's likeness in a public or online space. Be sure you adhere to the student's and family's wishes with regard to the information you then distribute to the remaining classroom community members.

Once you have obtained the information you intend to share, and have secured the necessary permissions, you can share the student of the week details in a manner and structure conducive to your online classroom needs. You might post the information to a classroom community homepage, email the information through a weekly course newsletter or online bulletin, or promote the student of the week through dialogue at the opening of a synchronous class meeting. As you proceed in the coming weeks and months, be sure to reference what you have learned in an effort to cultivate and maintain your own relationship with individual students, and in your efforts to encourage student-to-student connections within the online classroom.

STRATEGIES FOR MAINTAINING CONNECTIONS AND RELATIONSHIPS

Consistent Communication

Since virtual teachers don't have the opportunity to see students on a daily basis, it is important to establish consistent communication if you want to foster and maintain positive relationships. A key to establishing such communication is setting guidelines and expectations from the start of the course. What is the most effective means of contacting each student? Does the student and family prefer phone, email, text, or video conferencing? What are your designated office hours for student contact and support? What are your agreed-upon expectations for maintaining communication with one another?

It can be challenging to maintain open communication within an asynchronous environment. However, it is important to keep the lines of communication open in an effort to provide learners academic support, as well as cultivate positive relationships throughout the duration of the online course.

Weekly News

Once you have established a foundation for community, it is imperative to find ways to maintain connections with and between students. Introductions are essential, but they are never enough. Traditional classrooms provide opportunities for regular, consistent communication and connection. Students can share the ups and downs of their day-to-day lives, support one another through life's challenges, and relish in celebrating each other's accomplishments. Such connections are just as important for online learners, but more challenging to maintain.

Sharing weekly news is one strategy for maintaining open communication and connection with online learners. As you reach out and speak with your students, ask about their lives outside of academics. Do they have any good news to share with you and with their peers? Is there anything they want you to know and/or share with others? For instance, if your student is active in a local sport, how is that going for them? Have they played any recent games or celebrated a recent championship? Do they have a birthday or special event coming up that they would like others to know about? Have they accomplished any recent goals?

As you learn more about the lives and experiences of your students, take time to share such accomplishments and news with the class. For example, if your learning management system provides space to share an opening screen or slideshow, you might choose to craft slides that display student news or photos. If you send out a weekly newsletter to students or families, you can designate space within the newsletter to share news of student life events and celebrations.

The key is to maintain open communication and utilize that communication to continue learning and connecting with your students. In celebrating student success and sharing such success with fellow students, you can strive to maintain positive relationships and social emotional development for adolescent online learners.

Chapter Two

Motivating Readers and Writers in the Online Classroom

Everyone could use a little motivation now and again. Whether it's a friendly nudge to try something new, motivation to get up, dust off, and press on toward a specific goal, or even the inclination to finish something we started long ago, sometimes a little motivation can go a long way. The same can be said for our online learners as they begin, immerse, engage, and press forward in their online learning.

It is no surprise that motivation is key to learning and engagement in the middle- and secondary-level classroom (Ryan & Deci, 2000). However, online learning often requires a higher degree of self-motivation than the traditional classroom (Potts, 2019). Student motivation can serve as a driving force in the online learner's choice to log in and actively engage in reading and writing activities through persistent effort and focus within the learning process (Vanslambrouck et al., 2017). When online courses do not meet the pedagogical needs or expectations of learners, students can become increasingly dissatisfied and disengaged from their learning (Rovai, 2003).

Students must see value in the academic task, and believe they can achieve success if they are to find the motivation to actively engage and learn. Literacy research informs us that student attention and motivation to read and write decreases around middle school (Hogan, 1980) and continues to do so as students progress through their schooling (Guthrie & Wigfield, 2000). Reading and writing are crucial to every aspect of a student's academic career (and beyond). As such, it is imperative that virtual teachers consider a variety of variables and forms of engagement when working with online learners (Hobson & Puruhito, 2018).

To encourage online learners toward engagement, there are three specific types of motivation that become important to address: behavioral, cognitive, and emotional (Fredricks et al., 2004). According to Fredricks, Blumenfeld, and Paris (2004), behavioral engagement focuses on student involvement in learning tasks and the online classroom environment, cognitive engagement refers to the use of effective learning strategies, and emotional engagement refers to the students' emotional responses to the learning tasks and online classroom environment. As you identify effective means of encouraging behavioral, cognitive, and emotional motivation within your students, you open the door to effective reading and writing instruction in the online classroom.

STRATEGIES FOR MOTIVATING STUDENTS IN THE VIRTUAL CLASSROOM

Motivating Behavioral Engagement

Signing into class is the first step toward active learning. Yet it is this very step that can serve as one of the most challenging pieces of virtual education for adolescent learners. Behavioral engagement gives attention to time on task. Unlike a traditional classroom, the online learning platform has the potential to limit social presence, or a person's ability to establish a presence in the moment. In the traditional classroom, teachers can work to motivate and engage learners in the day's activities through proximity and face-to-face contact. However, the asynchronous nature of the online classroom significantly limits a teacher's ability to actively encourage learners to log in and engage in lessons. For this reason, we begin with a list of strategies for motivating learners to sign in and engage in literacy activities with regularity and consistency.

Formulating an Engagement Plan Together

Adolescent learners crave autonomy. They want to feel a sense of control over their own learning. However, the asynchronous nature of some online learning puts more independent control on the shoulders of students than what they might encounter within a traditional classroom setting. At times, this level of independence can be daunting or challenging for students. There is a risk that students will deviate from a prescribed plan of action, and fail to consistently sign in to their online course.

It is important to create space for virtual learners to have a voice in crafting a plan of engagement that will work for them. You want to assist students in facilitating a plan that accounts for their unique needs and goals. Rather than dictating a uniform plan of engagement, you can work with students and families to craft a plan that works for them. Such a plan should include action steps to encourage consistency in the frequency and depth of active course engagement and progress. Some suggested questions that can be addressed in an engagement plan include:

- When will the learner log in to the course throughout the week?
- What goals can the learner set and seek to achieve through regular effort and focus?
- When can the instructor and student engage in synchronous communication to provide additional support, instruction, and ongoing reflection?

The key is for the teacher and the student to formulate a plan together to ensure the student is responsible for consistent effort and attention to course material, instruction, and assessment.

As the course progresses, continue to revisit, revise, and reflect on the initial plan of engagement. Work together to ensure all stakeholders have a voice and contribute to ensuring consistency in engagement and learning. Instructors want to avoid micromanaging student engagement, while finding ways to motivate online learners to grow in their ability to self-manage and take responsibility for entering, engaging, and successfully progressing through the course. Establishing an initial plan is the first step in achieving this goal.

Consistent Communication

In chapter 1, we shared ways of initiating contact to ensure ongoing communication with learners and families for the duration of the online course. Establishing contact is only the beginning. If teachers hope to encourage students to consistently sign in and engage in course material, you must also find ways to maintain communication throughout the semester or year. Students should view teachers as active participants in their learning process. You want them to know you are there to provide support and encouragement. If students fail to view you as active members in their learning process, you run the risk of limiting your ability to encourage regular active engagement in the online space. Consistent communication can take many forms. Below we offer some suggested forms of communication.

Weekly newsletter. Virtual Teachers might establish and share a weekly course newsletter via email or online posts. This newsletter can include general updates or highlights from the course, as well as individual updates on learner progress. For example, instructors can design a newsletter that contains a mail-merge section in which the teacher shares updates on the individual learner's assignment completion, course grade, and frequency of online engagement. This simple checkpoint can do wonders for helping learners and families maintain awareness of the frequency and progress of their online activity and motivate students to push forward in their regular engagement with the class. It might serve as validation for learners who are consistently signing in to their online course and moving forward in coursework, as well as an early alert for those who may have fallen back in terms of consistent engagement.

Weekly office hours. Teachers can also hold weekly office hours within a virtual learning platform. Sign into your online class space, and let students know you are available to provide support and feedback. Try to coordinate your hours in a way that works for your needs, as well as the availability of students and families. Ensure your hours are consistent. This way, students know they can count on you to be accessible at a predetermined day and time each week. This simple step in consistency can work wonders in motivating students to sign in and meet with you for necessary academic support. When they know you are consistent in your availability to support their academic endeavors, they can find greater motivation for seeking out help.

Phone call. A phone call or text can work wonders in encouraging students to sign in and move forward in their online learning. Set aside time each week to initiate calls with learners who might benefit from additional external motivation to sign in to their online course. Or, reach out as a consistent check-in to remind students that you are present and available to provide instructional support. A simple text stating, "Hi! Just checking in to see how you're doing this week. How are things going with lesson ____?" provides a sense of immediacy often lacking in the asynchronous environment. Let students know when you observe their absence. It is important that they understand their lack of behavioral engagement is felt within the classroom. Let them know that you care, you want to see them succeed, and you are concerned when they don't sign in. When students know you are present, aware, and available, they receive a level of behavioral motivation that might otherwise be missing from the online classroom setting.

Communication log. No matter which form of communication you find works best for you and your online students, be sure to maintain records regarding your communication with learners and families over the duration of the course. Keep track of communication tendencies, frequency, and details from each successful encounter. Who have you had a chance to communicate with this week? What method of contact did you utilize (e.g., email, phone call, text, video conferencing)? Who have you been trying to reach without immediate success? A communication log can assist you in maintaining key information on student progress and engagement, as well as help you identify areas of communicative need with regard to establishing and maintaining contact with learners and families.

Motivating Cognitive Engagement

Once you find effective ways of motivating learners to log in to the course, it's essential that we identify ways to motivate them in maintaining active engagement and cognitive growth. It can be easy to sign in, move through the motions, and simply progress for the sake of finishing the online program. Your goal is to motivate your students to think beyond speed and completion. Rather, you want to find ways of motivating students to engage at a critical level. Teachers want students to seek out content mastery and high-skill performance. For this reason, you need to identify ways to encourage cognitive engagement throughout your students' enrollment and engagement with your online class.

Activating Background Knowledge

The first step in motivating cognitive engagement is allowing students to connect new information to known information. You want to assist them in building on their schema—or current level of knowledge and understanding. In an effort to achieve this goal, it is important to look back on the information you shared and acquired during your initial and ongoing connections with the online learner (see chapter 1). As you press forward in developing your content and classroom structure, you must first be aware of what your students already know, believe, and understand. In addition to building from your knowledge of student interest, hobbies, abilities, and needs, you can utilize a wide variety of pre-assessments to gauge student understanding and mastery of course content and skills in your effort to motivate and engage students.

Providing Student Choice

Adolescent learners need to be heard and understood. They need a voice in their individual learning. Research on student choice about reading and writing in the traditional classroom has found that choice increases the likelihood students will engage more in these literacy practices. In virtual classrooms, student choice is also a highly motivating factor for cognitive engagement. When students can find personal interest and purpose to their work, they are more inclined to actively engage in the curriculum. Providing choice helps students to find enjoyment and purpose within their content-area learning.

There are multiple ways virtual teachers can infuse student choice into the online classroom. Virtual teachers can provide student choice in course content, process, and product. While it may not always be appropriate or feasible to promote choice in all three ways for every lesson, it is important to seek out ways to provide options as a means of differentiating online curriculum, as well as cognitive engagement for our students.

Choice in content (online sources for books, articles, magazines, websites). One of the key advantages to engaging in an online course is the sheer number of resources available at your fingertips! While teachers might have limited access to some resources in the traditional classroom environment, the virtual space can provide students and teachers access to a plethora of books, articles, websites, and more. For this reason, virtual teachers can be encouraged to consider implementing student choice in supplemental course materials. For instance, instead of requiring all learners to download and read a single text (much like the use of a whole-class novel in the traditional classroom space), virtual educators can provide students with choices in selecting a text that best addresses a noted content-area standard or skill set. If learners are engaging in research and writing, virtual educators can provide space for students to choose the resources and supports that best meet the requirements for the assignment, while allowing students the opportunity to learn more about a topic that speaks to their own interests and needs. In chapter 3, we will share more specific ways virtual educators can implement student choice in content as a means of assisting online learners forge their individual reader and writer identities.

Choice in process (differentiating how you approach instruction). Another essential way to motivate online learners through choice is differentiation in process, or the method by which you approach online instruction. However, unlike differentiation of content, virtual educators might find themselves limited in terms of process for a variety of reasons. It might be that your institution restricts teacher control or voice in the development and implementation of course modules or instruction. Or, perhaps you know what works in terms of approach in the traditional space, but find limitations when infusing technology or particular programs and applications within instruction. Despite potential limitations, the key is to identify areas in which you can infuse choice into the instructional design and approach, and do so in ways that effectively motivate and meet the needs of the individual learner.

Teachers can strive to differentiate asynchronous instruction by approaching content through a variety of technological channels. Online applications are designed to promote learning through visual, auditory, and kinesthetic means. Some applications might draw in the attention and engagement of some learners more so than others. And, some applications are more appropriate to the purpose and abilities of some students than others. As you research the myriad of applications available to you and your students, take time to consider the following:

- How will this application address your content or lesson objectives?
- How will this application meet the academic, social, and emotional needs of your learners?

- How will this application motivate your learners to engage and excel in the course?
- Is this application accessible for your learners?
- Does this application represent the level of quality learning and development you hope to see your learners achieve?

In addition to the use of online applications, virtual teachers can differentiate instruction within synchronous platforms. Research demonstrates how online learners are more motivated to actively engage in their learning when they identify a sense of immediacy and connection with the teacher. A virtual learning platform, or learning management system (LMS), provides space for teachers to engage with learners in real time. Teachers can utilize such platforms to provide direct instruction, collaborative group learning, as well as one-on-one tutoring and instructional support. Just as in a traditional classroom, virtual teachers can engage students in synchronous instruction that adapts to meet the individual learner's needs. In chapter 3, we share specific instructional methods and supports that virtual educators can use to advance student learning and literacy.

Choice in product. A final area in which virtual teachers can strive to implement student choice lies within assessment. In the traditional classroom, teachers utilize formal assessment structures (e.g., quizzes, tests, essays) as well as creative assessments (e.g., projects, presentations, collaborative assessment) to determine student progress and mastery of content. But choice in assessment does not have to be limited to the traditional classroom environment. Students in virtual classrooms can also demonstrate formation and mastery of learning through a variety of assessment structures. By uncovering ways students can have choice in determining the technological means by which they will demonstrate their understanding, teachers can further motivate online learners to fully engage in asynchronous or synchronous assessment. In chapter 8, we share a variety of assessment techniques for assessing student reading engagement and development. In chapter 11, we share assessment strategies designed to meet writing objectives within the virtual classroom.

Making Learning Meaningful and Relevant

In addition to accounting for student voice within the curriculum, instruction, and assessment, virtual teachers need to ensure learning is meaningful and relevant. The online space provides a platform for students to reach a worldwide audience. When learning extends beyond the confines of the classroom walls, students can find motivation to give their work added effort and focus. Providing learners opportunities to share their understanding and work with a wider audience brings authenticity to the learning process. Throughout this book, we provide important considerations and practical strategies that virtual teachers can utilize to encourage students to learn and share their work with an audience beyond the immediate classroom community. Authenticity leads to greater cognitive motivation.

Motivating Emotional Engagement

Students who enter a classroom don't leave their social and emotional needs at the door. Rather, teachers are tasked with reaching and teaching the whole child each and every day. The same is true for online students. Our learners log into the classroom with a world of emotions, personal needs, and expectations. In fact, unlike the traditional student who may see school as a means of escape or safety in an otherwise turbulent world, many online learners lack a physical distance from their social, emotional, mental, and physical challenges. They may log in while lying ill in a hospital bed, sitting inside a juvenile detention facility, seeking treatment for a behavioral need, or caring for a sibling at home.

In addition, when learners fail to see and maintain an emotional connection to their online learning environment and class community, they may fail to find the internal motivation to consistently and actively engage at a high level of learning. The reality of online learning is the clear separation in time and space. Teachers can't always see virtual learners as they engage in the online course. For this reason, it is imperative to strive to identify new ways of motivating virtual students on an emotional level. After establishing a connection with learners (see chapter 1), it is important to capitalize on such connections to further motivate students.

Capitalizing on Connections and Relationships

The first step in cultivating emotional motivation is establishing a personal and significant connection with virtual learners. In chapter 1, we shared strategies for establishing such a connection across the asynchronous platform. Once a connection is established, the key is to continue fostering the relationship and identifying ways to capitalize on the connection in all aspects of the course. Utilize the strategies from chapter 1 to maintain awareness of individual student interests, experiences, needs, talents, and abilities. Be certain to consider the unique identities and needs of your learners as you create, refine, and diversify elements of your online course and instruction. Virtual learners should never feel that they are simply another name on your classroom roster. They need to feel valued and connected despite the obvious distance within the virtual platform. As students discover that you are aware and considerate of their lives both inside and outside the online space, they will be more inclined to fully engage, reach out for help, and make progress in their coursework.

Promoting Self-Efficacy

Pushing ourselves to keep trying when we encounter challenges or failure is crucial to growth, development, and success. A growth mindset is critical for learners. But for students to find success, they need to believe they can reach success. Students need a positive sense of self-efficacy—the belief in their ability to be successful—to acquire a high degree of emotional motivation. In addition to capitalizing on relationships, teachers should identify ways they might encourage students as they navigate through the online classroom.

When engaging in synchronous instruction, virtual teachers can utilize many of the same techniques for encouraging learners to press forward, try again, or challenge their thinking to reach a higher level of understanding. Teachers can verbally respond to demonstrated needs during synchronous instruction, and can utilize chat boxes, text messages, and phone calls to offer words of encouragement and celebration. But how might teachers continue to promote student self-efficacy when lacking the immediacy of the moment?

Given the often asynchronous nature of online learning, it can be challenging to provide a word of encouragement and praise at the moment a student struggles to proceed with a course module or assignment. Therefore, teachers must utilize strategies that adapt our in-the-moment approaches to encouraging the emotional motivation of online learners. While a positive email, text, or letter home can cause a smile, you want to find ways to encourage student-generated means of self-efficacy. You want to help students identify their own strengths, development, and success within their course engagement, progress, and learning.

For instance, instead of taking all the responsibility for sharing updates and student progress checks with learners and families, encourage students to identify and share their own development. Have students compose a weekly newsletter or blog post to share with their guardians. Students can highlight their progress within the course modules, share something that stood out to them within their academic engagement this week, and identify personal goals for next week. If they feel they did not progress as they expected, encourage them to reflect on how they can take steps to move forward next week. How can they seek out assistance when they need it? How might they take this week's challenges, and transform them into steps for progress?

Encourage learners to set a weekly goal and identify steps toward accomplishing their unique goal. In taking time to reflect on their active engagement and individual progress, students can view themselves as successful in working toward individual goals. They can identify setbacks as opportunities for growth. In addition, students can work with you to establish checkpoints toward mastery. Allowing students to take charge of their progress and learning, and helping them to view themselves as successful learners, can go a long way to encouraging motivation and consistent engagement.

Chapter Three

Uncovering Reading and Writing Identities

Every individual represents a compilation of identity markers. If we take a moment to unpack our identity, and strive to share how we define ourselves, we would likely share out markers such as our gender identity, race, culture, social identities, and more. In addition, we could include academic markers that represent our self-perceptions as educators and learners. Two such considerations are how we define ourselves as readers and writers.

All content areas require students to read and write. The practice of these literacies is crucial not only in helping students come to learn and develop content knowledge, but will be necessary for all aspects of life in school and beyond. However, more often than not, student perceptions of their ability to read and write have been largely influenced by the ability to pass state-mandated assessments—assessments that define literacy as an act or event. But literacy is so much more. Literacy encompasses cognitive, linguistic, social, and developmental processes in both what is learned and what is practiced (Kucer, 2009). In other words, literacy is both an act and an identity.

Reading identity refers to how capable individuals believe they are in comprehending texts, and the value they place on reading and their understanding of what it means to be a particular type of reader (Hall, 2012). The same holds true for writing identity (Ivanic, 1998). While teachers often come to know their students' reading and writing identities through observations and the students' own voices, in online classrooms you lose the ability to "hear" and "see" students share these identities. So how do virtual teachers discover student reading and writing identities in the online classroom? More importantly, how do you help students develop their own reading and writing identities in a positive manner?

Literacy as a practice connects directly to a person's beliefs, values, and attitudes, and changes over time as the person continues to use literacy to learn (Seban & Tavsanli, 2015). As such, it is important that virtual teachers not only uncover their students' identities as readers and writers, but that they also find ways to encourage students to build positive literacy identities. But before you can achieve this, you must explore your students' literacy landscapes. Teachers must discover how students identify as readers and writers.

STRATEGIES FOR ASSISTING STUDENTS IN UNCOVERING AND STRENGTHENING THEIR LITERACY IDENTITIES

Students' reading and writing identities are often influenced by a series of factors: their socioeconomic status, their peers, their family dynamics, their schools (both prior and current), their personal interests, and even their belief systems (religion). In schools where educators have listened to students' voices and developed instructional practices that help students develop literacy identities, great improvements in students' literacy have been made (Allen, 2000). Because there is distance between teacher and students in online classrooms, finding a way to capture the student voice is imperative. There are several strategies that a virtual teacher can implement to accomplish this goal within the online classroom.

Reading and Writing Survey

One strategy that virtual teachers can utilize to assess their students' experiences and attitudes toward reading and writing, and help inform and direct content-area reading and writing curriculum, is a reading and writing survey. This survey should include questions about students' reading and writing interests, and inquire about their least favorite types of reading and writing. In doing so, virtual teachers can come to learn how their students view themselves as readers and writers, while giving teachers information that can help motivate each student. There are several popular surveys that are often used in the traditional classroom that can also be used in the virtual classroom, such as Linda Rief's Reading-Writing Survey (Rief, 1991) and Pernille Ripp's Reading Identity Challenge Survey (see www.pernillesripp.com). While pre-generated reading and writing surveys are easy and accessible, virtual teachers may want to create their own surveys specific to their content.

For example, in addition to general questions about a student's reading and writing preferences, science teachers could pose questions such as: *How do you feel about writing lab reports? What topics in science do you enjoy reading about? Do you watch movies or TV shows about science? If so, which ones? What types of activities do you like to complete in science (read science books, conduct experiments, watch science videos, create models, etc.)*? Math teachers could pose similar questions, such as: *How do you feel about writing in math? Do visuals help you learn math? Describe the reading and writing strategies you use to better help you understand math.*

Reading and Writing Confessional Video

As mentioned earlier in this chapter, reading and writing identities are often shaped by attitudes and beliefs our students hold about literacy. Confessionals, or the act of confessing, can offer teachers great insight into students' beliefs and attitudes toward reading and writing, while also offering students an opportunity to really reflect on their own literacy identities.

There are two ways that a student can approach a reading and writing confessional. In the first approach, teachers prompt students to record a video confession of their attitudes and beliefs about reading and writing in their content area. For example, a social studies teacher might ask students to record a confessional about reading history. They may ask the student about reading history textbooks, or maps, or primary documents. Or the teacher may even prompt the student to discuss what type of reading and writing activities in their content area support the student's reading and writing strengths.

The second approach draws on student choice (see chapter 2). Teachers could ask students to confess their beliefs and attitudes about reading and writing in general, or in their content area. Leaving this open for students to interpret not only provides choice in what a student wants to share with you—which motivates and engages the student—it also allows virtual teachers to come to know which aspects of reading and writing the student values.

Literary Legends

Literary legends provide a means of helping students become more aware of their reading and writing habits, while also providing important information that can help teachers motivate learners to develop their reading and writing skills. Ask students to chronicle what they have read and written in the last 30 days. You can specifically ask them to reference your content area, or you can ask them to record everything they read and write. Remind them that reading and writing involves more than just print text. Students should record visual reading (movies, YouTube videos, Snapchat videos, etc.), auditory reading (music, podcasts, etc.), lyrical writing (poems, songs, etc.), visual writing (photos, creation of Snapchat and YouTube videos, etc.), communicative writing (Instagram, Facebook, letters, etc.), reflective writing (journals), and any other forms of reading and writing that are relevant to them.

As teachers, we need to be able to draw on our students' reading and writing identities to engage and motivate them to practice these literacies. Beyond the sharing of these literary legends as a way to get to know your students' reading and writing identities, the virtual teacher can utilize this legend to further assist students in uncovering other reading and writing identity attributes. Additionally, legends can be used to further develop student literacy identities as virtual teachers make curricular decisions around classroom texts and approaches to reading and writing.

Virtual Chalk Talk

Traditionally, a chalk talk is a strategy in which the teacher poses a series of questions, words, or images on sheets of chart paper and places these sheets around the classroom. Students navigate throughout the room and silently share their thoughts, questions, connections, or anecdotes by writing or illustrating on each of the provided charts. Learners then respond to the ideas shared by a classmate in a visual or written form. Rather than converse aloud, students engage in conversation within text or image.

Virtual educators can transfer this engaging activity to the virtual space within online learning management systems. For instance, a teacher can create distinct "breakout rooms" within Blackboard Collaborate, and pose a statement, question, or image within each room. Students can then navigate between rooms to contribute to the silent online discussion. In tying this activity to uncovering reading and writing identities, the teacher can place terms such as "reader," "writer," "books," and "text" within each of the breakout rooms. Or, the teacher might ask students to paste an image that represents their current views about the noted terms or ideas within each space.

The teacher can initiate ideas with incomplete statements such as "When I think of writing, I feel . . ." or "Reading reminds me of . . ." and ask students to complete the phrase with a word, statement, or image that best represents their identity or thoughts regarding the reading and writing process. In utilizing a chalk talk approach to sharing out reading or writing identities, students not only have an opportunity to reveal their current thoughts, experiences, and feelings with regard to literacy, but also an opportunity to collaborate, connect, and experience the identities of their virtual classmates.

HELPING STUDENTS DEVELOP THEIR LITERACY IDENTITIES

Setting Literacy Goals

As described in chapter 2, motivation and engagement are keys to student learning in the middle and secondary classroom (Ryan & Deci, 2000). Setting literacy goals is a great way for students to not only reflect on their own literacy practices, but also motivate them to engage in these practices at more challenging levels. Through the setting of literacy goals, students take control of their literacy development.

Literacy goals can be short-term or long-term in nature. For example, a student might set a short-term goal of reading one book (of their choosing) by the end of the semester, or a long-term goal of reading three books (of their choosing) by the end of the school year. But no matter the length, in order for students' literacy goals to be effective, they must meet three criteria: they are meaningful, measurable, and attainable.

Because setting effective goals requires specific characteristics, it may be beneficial for virtual teachers to model this process for students. One way to accomplish this is for the virtual teacher to create and post a video of themselves walking through each attribute in crafting their own reading and writing goals. Another way to ensure that students meet the criteria of effective goal setting can be through the use of a graphic organizer (see figure 3.1).

While the setting of goals is a personal act, in the virtual classroom, it can be beneficial for students to share these goals with teachers. Teachers can

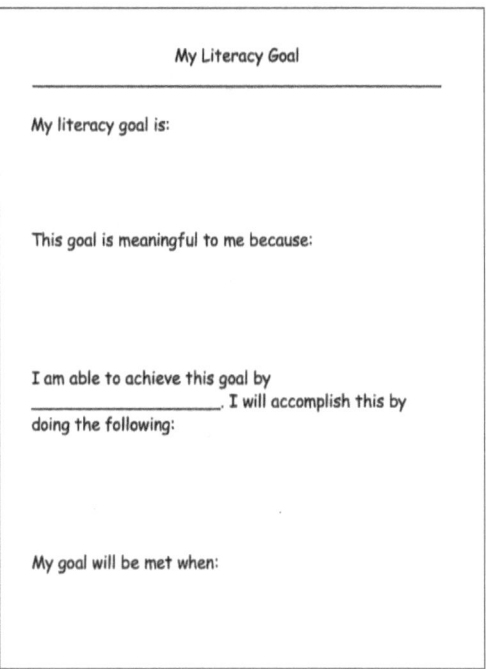

Figure 3.1. Setting literacy goals graphic organizer. *Created by the authors*

then use this information in meetings with students as a way to monitor their progress toward meeting their goals. Additionally, through sharing their literacy goals, students become more accountable for reaching them.

Student Choice

In chapter 2, we noted the value of providing opportunities for student choice to motivate and engage online learners. Providing space for student choice also allows teachers to learn more about student reading and writing identities, as well as further equipping learners to develop a positive perspective of their abilities as readers and writers. As virtual teachers monitor student text selections, writing approaches, and individual written work, they can gain greater insight into student preference, sense of self-efficacy, and self-perception regarding interests and abilities.

The virtual classroom provides a wide array of opportunities for student choice, if approached and implemented in a way that values and supports such opportunities. For instance, students have access to a myriad of texts and mediums. Such access can allow teachers the chance to infuse student voice within the daily curriculum and course content. Rather than engage in consistent, uniform reading and writing context and assignments, virtual teachers can empower learners to conduct quality online searches for texts, prompts, and writing approaches that interest and impact them on a personal level. When students feel empowered to flex their autonomy in the classroom, they are more likely to engage and allow their personal reading and writing identities to grow.

Chapter Four

Getting Ready to Read and Write

Readers and writers approach each unique text with a wealth of knowledge and experience. We encounter and craft stories and information through active interaction. Readers and writers are not empty vessels. Rather, our students bring funds of knowledge, or individual resources and strengths, to every literacy practice and engagement. They carry a rich tradition of literacy and understanding that, if acknowledged and built upon, can help them become more successful in developing and furthering their literacy engagement.

It is important that teachers avoid assumptions about students' funds of knowledge, background understanding, or current skills with regard to their level of readiness. Some research suggests that such assumptions are erroneous and that learning is influenced as much by students' prior knowledge as by the new instruction they receive. Attention, then, needs to be paid to this fundamental aspect of the learning process. Teachers need to identify ways to utilize all the knowledge and skills virtual learners bring to the table, rather than jumping headfirst into instruction that either ignores students' expertise, or propels them into a state of confusion or disconnection.

If learning begins where the students are and with what they know, then developing literacy and the sequence of literacy activities a teacher will implement should also begin there. Research informs us that we can jump-start learning by accessing pre-existing attitudes, experiences, and knowledge (Anderson, 1994; Taboada & Guthrie, 2004)—in other words, tapping students' background knowledge. This allows us to bridge the gap between what is being taught and what is already known in order to move students forward in their learning and literacy development.

STRATEGIES FOR TAPPING BACKGROUND KNOWLEDGE

Asynchronous

Know-Want-Learn-How

No matter the learning context, it is imperative that teachers uncover the knowledge that students bring with them to the classroom about content-specific topics and concepts. For one, tapping background knowledge allows the teacher to gauge where to begin their teaching. It also allows teachers to clear up any misconceptions that students may have. One strategy commonly utilized in most traditional content-area classrooms to accomplish this is Know-Want-Learn (KWL). The KWL strategy provides a framework for learning that can be used across content areas to help students become active constructors of meaning (Ogle, 1986). It elicits students' prior knowledge of the topic of the text, sets a purpose for learning, and helps students to monitor their comprehension. But since its introduction in 1986, the need for students to move toward critical thinking calls for a shift in how this strategy is implemented.

The traditional KWL graphic organizer contains three columns. The first column, "Know," asks students to record what they know about a specific topic. The second column, "Want," asks students to record what they want to know about the topic. And the third column, "Learn," prompts students to record what they learned throughout the unit/lesson on the topic. While the use of these three columns reflects student background knowledge and the development of new knowledge, we suggest that teachers add an additional H column, "How," to move students forward in their thinking.

In order for this strategy to be effective—for both students and teachers—there is a clear starting point. Before a teacher asks students to complete this graphic organizer, they should inform students what the end product or task of the unit will be. In other words, students should know what mastery of the standard(s) being taught looks like. Knowing this creates a new approach to and new meaning for each column in the KWLH.

After providing students the topic that will be explored in the unit and what mastery will look like (what they are expected to do with the information learned), ask students to complete the "Know" column. Once completed, ask students to complete the "Want" column by prompting them to list/record what they still need to learn in order to complete the final task and demonstrate mastery of understanding. As students work through the lesson, they should then record the new information learned in the "Learn" column. At the end of the lesson, prior to demonstration of mastery, ask students to review their KWL notes. If there is still information needed, ask them to record what this information is and where they could go to discover it in the "How" column.

Because this strategy involves several components, we suggest that virtual teachers ask students to keep a copy of the graphic organizer in a shared folder, or on Google Docs, so the teacher can continually monitor the students' learning.

Virtual Walks

The virtual context provides access to a world of information in a matter of seconds. Virtual walks are a terrific way to encourage background reflection and learning in preparation for a new topic or text in the classroom. To start, identify topics significant to understanding the background and context of the text/story. After students have an opportunity to consider what they already know about each topic, help them to research and learn more through teacher- or student-generated virtual walks. Essentially, you want to create a document or presentation that links students to informational websites and videos pertaining to each topic. You may initiate this activity by creating a virtual walk of your own. Select credible, accessible resources that enhance student background on topics you have identified to be significant to their comprehension of the text. Provide questions or opportunity for targeted note taking along the way. Students can access the resources in an asynchronous fashion, but should maintain contact with you and/or their peers to ensure active engagement and understanding.

Once students have experience engaging in a virtual walk, you can find ways of empowering learners to contribute to a collaborative virtual walk, or create one of their own. For instance, you can explicitly teach students how to identify credible versus false information online. Then, provide students a topic related to their identified area of expertise and/or related to a key background focus of the text, and encourage them to identify virtual resources they would like to share with classmates. Putting the ownership of the virtual walk in the hands of the students not only encourages them to share their unique funds of knowledge and experience, but motivates them to actively seek out additional background information and support their virtual classmates along the way. Virtual walks encourage students to build on their current understanding of textual context, while initiating understanding of concepts that are new or foundational to reading comprehension and engagement.

Video/Voice Responses

In the brick-and-mortar classroom, teachers have the ability to see and hear their students in person. They can observe student facial expressions and body movements, and note tone in responses as a way to gauge students' self-reported knowledge of a concept or topic. Because virtual classrooms are separated by time and space, observing students becomes more complex for virtual teachers, especially in an asynchronous setting. One way that virtual teachers can tap into students' background knowledge, while also having an opportunity to see and observe them, is through video or voice responses.

In this strategy, virtual teachers simply ask students to tell them what they know about a specific topic or concept. Ask students to share their responses through a technology application such as Flipgrid or VoiceThread, or to create a video using their phone or computer camera function. No matter what medium students choose to complete the task, it is imperative that they upload the video or voice response as a way of assisting virtual teachers in gaining a deeper understanding of what knowledge each student brings to the classroom.

Synchronous

Anticipation Guides

Anticipation guides serve as a powerful tool for identifying significant themes relevant to a classroom text, and providing learners insight into a text prior to the reading of the story. Teachers preview a text, and identify statements pertaining to the story that are likely to generate student conversation and promote reflection about the individual's current beliefs, attitudes, perspectives, and experiences. For instance, an anticipation guide for S. E. Hinton's *The Outsiders* (1967), a young adult title commonly utilized in middle-level classrooms, may contain statements such as "Adults often believe negative stereotypes about teenagers," "Friends can be family," or "We are all viewed as equals in the eyes of the law." Each statement relates to important events and characters from the story, provides an opportunity for students to tap into their background knowledge of essential concepts to the text, serves as a way of activating a student's own perceptions and experiences, and enhances a student's motivation to engage in reading the novel. Students take time to either "agree" or "disagree" with each statement, and then prepare to share out their individual thoughts or reactions with the class. Why do they agree? Why do they disagree? How might each statement relate to the story they are about to encounter?

Virtual teachers can transfer anticipation guides from the traditional classroom to the virtual context with minimal time or effort. There are a multitude of online word processing and document sharing programs that provide space to simply type up an anticipation guide and share it out with virtual learners. The key to this activity lies in the space it provides for peer-to-peer conversation and interaction. We want to activate student understanding through self-reflection, but also engage students in collaborative interpretation through active conversation.

As a virtual teacher, you can utilize your online management system or synchronous conferencing programs, like those shared in previous chapters, to engage learners in open conversation around their unique perspectives for each statement. Just ensure that students approach this conversation in a space that is safe, respectful, and inclusive of diverse experiences and identities. Traditionally, anticipation guides contain statements designed to really evoke connection and critical discussion—not elicit a single, anticipated response. As such, students need to feel that they are safe to engage with one another regarding their own views, they must be respectful of ideas that diverge from their own beliefs, and need to be open to examining things in a way they haven't before. In utilizing strategies shared in chapter 1, and setting standards for community conversation, virtual teachers can ensure open, reflective discussion of themes to be encountered within the text. In addition, it's important to take note of what students share within their response to the anticipation guide, and in conversation with classmates. Seek out ways to identify areas where student response provides insight into each child's current funds of knowledge and background understanding of the text. You can utilize this insight in developing course curriculum and navigating students through their unique reading of the selected title.

Consistent Check-ins

Formative assessment requires consistency in monitoring and evaluating student growth and development. Just as teachers in the traditional classroom consistently observe and identify students' different levels of understanding, it is important that virtual teachers maintain awareness of student comprehension, preparation, and confusion. You want to ensure clarity in content and instruction. You want to know that virtual learners are comprehending course material, and that they are prepared to engage with texts at a deep, critical level.

A simple check-in can do wonders for assessing student progress and contextual understanding. A phone call, text, or online chat can provide space for teachers to informally assess student learning, and give students an opportunity to seek out clarification as needed. Simply put, virtual teachers should find a way to check in and ensure students are on track with their learning and progress as they move forward in course content.

THE IMPORTANCE OF DEVELOPING VOCABULARY AND CONCEPT KNOWLEDGE

Concepts are ideas we have about something based on our understanding of its characteristics. We label concepts with words. Together, these become our vocabulary. Students enter the classroom with background knowledge of vocabulary. Some students may have a deep understanding of content vocabulary, while others may have had little experience with the words and concepts, or may even hold misconceptions about their meaning. Because word knowledge is an essential cueing system for comprehension, failure to understand even a few words can impede comprehension and learning. If a student does not know the meanings of a sufficient number of the words in a text, then comprehension is impossible.

Comprehending a word is more than just being able to remember its meaning. Exposing students to words and definitions and asking them to memorize them does not help students understand a word. Rather, students must be engaged in practice with that word in order to discover and retain meaning (Harmon et al., 2000). Because words and concepts are discipline-specific, this practice belongs in every content area.

Below we share a number of strategies that virtual teachers can implement to help their students develop word and concept knowledge. However, before a teacher begins to utilize these strategies there are important steps that must occur:

- *Choose words and concepts judiciously.* If words appear in bold or italics in the text you are preparing your students to read, these do not need to be taught. Most textbooks will offer students the definition of these words in a legend somewhere on the page.
- *If a word appears in the text and it is preceded or followed by context clues, then the word does not need to be taught.* Students should be practicing using context clues to determine meaning as they read.
- *While a text may include several words that might be foreign to students, only choose the words and concepts that align with your purpose for reading or writing the text.* When we provide too many words, students can become overwhelmed and disconnected. The reading and writing then becomes about showing word meaning and less about coming to understand that word within the context of your content area topic and purpose.

STRATEGIES FOR DEVELOPING VOCABULARY AND CONCEPT KNOWLEDGE

Apps and Games

A quick online search will provide teachers and students a multitude of options regarding vocabulary development applications and games. Whether it is a multiplayer word-generating game, online crossword puzzle activity, or vocabulary instructional and assessment tool, the options are nearly limitless. Such applications and activities have the potential to engage virtual learners through social relevancy, humor, and fun! The key is identifying applications that speak to your objectives and content focus in the course curriculum. As we all know, not all apps are created equal. In searching for programs that meet the needs of your virtual students, consider the following questions:

- Is the application free and accessible?
- Does the application or game maintain the privacy of the user?
- Are there social or collaborative components that might be harmful, inappropriate, or harmful to my students' learning, motivation, or engagement?
- Does the application promote vocabulary development based on current research and educationally sound methods?
- Does the program provide space for scaffolding or individual progression based on the needs of my students?
- Is the program developmentally appropriate for the learners in my virtual classroom?

While these are simply a few suggested considerations, it is important to always review, reflect, and give careful thought to your intended objective in utilizing a select application or game, the context of your virtual classroom, and how the program will best meet the needs of your learners.

Vocabulary Rating Scales

If teachers want our students to read and write through the lens of a particular content area—as historians, scientists, mathematicians, or other specialists—then you need to equip students with content-area word knowledge. While students will gain word knowledge through incidental learning—hearing others use the word, or repeated encounters with the word in a variety of texts—the teaching of content-specific words and concepts should be approached through interactive pedagogy if you truly want students to come to know and use content vocabulary. One strategy that virtual teachers can implement in accomplishing this is the vocabulary rating scale (VRS).

The VRS is a strategy that utilizes a four-column graphic organizer that asks students to rate their understanding of content-specific words and concepts prior to reading. The columns are labeled "Word," "Know It Well," "Heard It," and "Don't Know It." The strategy requires students to rate their understanding of vocabulary listed in the "Word" column by placing a check mark or symbol in the corresponding column. However, having students tell you that they know what a word means is not sufficient evidence to prove they understand a word. Teachers need to discover exactly how a student defines a word in order to determine if they have the appropriate understanding necessary to use the word. By adding an additional step to this strategy, teachers can ensure that all students are working from the same vernacular, thus removing any vocabulary obstacles that could impede comprehension.

In transferring this strategy to the online classroom, there are several steps that a virtual teacher must take. The first, and most obvious, is to share the graphic organizer with the students. As mentioned above with the KWLH organizer, we suggest that the teacher posts the VRS organizer in a shared file so they can access it in order to monitor students' word and concept understanding. Before students begin to complete the graphic organizer, the second step requires the teacher to read the words aloud to the students. Virtual teachers can record the reading of the words via a video app or other apps such as Flipgrid and VoiceThread, and post on the course page for students to access. Once students listen to the teacher reading the words, prompt them to complete the graphic organizer. However, in addition to rating their understanding, ask students to provide a definition of each word. If students indicate that they "Know It Well," they should define the word. If they have "Heard It," have them indicate where they heard the word before and provide a definition. If students "Don't Know It," ask them to make a prediction of what the word means, drawing on the KWLH tapping background knowledge activity implemented in the lesson. This part of the strategy should be completed individually.

Once students rate and define each word, the next steps will require synchronous activities. First, teachers should pair or team students. Virtual teachers can create breakout rooms on the course page for team collaborations. In teams, students will share their definitions and collaborate to create a team definition for each word. In order to ensure that each team member is participating, virtual teachers should assign one team leader responsible for recording the team definition. We suggest that these definitions be recorded in Google Docs as a way for the teacher to monitor team progress. Additionally, the team leader should record the definitions using a different color font for each team member's contribution. This will guarantee that each team member contributed.

Once teams have crafted their definitions, it is time to share them with the whole class. This will require virtual teachers to assign a date and time for everyone to meet synchronously. Virtual teachers could ask students to meet via Zoom or through another video conferencing application. Prior to this meeting, the teacher should create a chart listing each word and their definitions that each team created. This chart should be easily accessible to students during the meeting. We suggest using Google Docs to accomplish this.

During the whole-class meeting, the teacher should go word by word, sharing each team's definition with students. It is important to give students time to read over each definition. Once read through, ask students to discuss the similarities and differences between the definitions. As the discussion unfolds, the teacher should keep a visible chart, outlining the similarities and differences the students identify. Once completed, the teacher should then ask students to craft a class definition for the word. Ask students to first draw on the similarities, and build from there. If there is important information missing from the definition, or the students are on the wrong track, the teacher can step in to redirect students. However, it is important that the teacher does not provide the definition; rather, the teacher leads students to discovery of meaning.

Once the class agrees on a final definition, the last step is for students to record the definition. Students can either record it on the graphic organizer, or in their course dictionary. A caution about creating a course dictionary: make sure that students aren't recording words and definitions alphabetically—these should be recorded per concept or topic instead.

Virtual Word Walls

Word walls are a popular method of tracking significant, new, or confusing vocabulary terms throughout a unit of study. Teachers and students contribute words, sentences, context, definitions, and/or images to accompany their reading and engagement with course content. Word walls offer a consistent way to provide visual reminders and connection to students' developing vocabulary. They provide context, repetition, and support. Students can reference the class word wall as they read, write, speak, and engage with course materials, texts, and assignments on a daily basis.

Virtual classrooms also hold potential for utilizing word walls and engaging students in more active vocabulary identification and development. While the virtual space may not have physical walls, you can utilize online platforms and programs to house word walls as they grow over the duration of the course. In fact, the virtual space allows for word walls to travel with students across space and time. For instance, teachers and students can utilize Google Slides, or a similar platform, to share vocabulary terms, phrases, links, and images for individual and group reference. Such platforms allow students to take ownership of their vocabulary development as they contribute terms, identify links they can follow for additional information, and paste images that relate to their understanding and use of each term. Students can reference the class word wall at any time, and teachers can reference the word wall during one-on-one correspondence with learners, or during synchronous instruction.

Creating Word Memes

Let's face it, students love memes! Teachers love memes! We all enjoy a good meme now and again. Memes, derived from an element of culture or behavior that is passed from one individual to another, have become commonplace within our ever-evolving technological world. Virtual users pass along images, videos, and slang that capture current social trends, activities, and mindsets. Memes offer a lot of potential in identifying, sharing, and developing student vocabulary while providing space for students to cut loose and have a little fun in the process.

To begin, virtual teachers can work with students to identify current meme trends. What's popular? What's trending? Begin simply by connecting with students and providing them space to share out their current experience and understanding of memes and meme culture. After all, learners often carry a level of expertise and current awareness of social trends in ways that exceed our own understanding and engagement.

Then, identify vocabulary of relevance and significance to the current course material. What terms are new? Are there particular words that stand out as challenging, important, or unique to the task or text at hand? You might select terminology in advance, or provide students space to identify terms they would like to utilize for the purpose of the meme activity.

Finally, provide time and opportunity for students to work independently or with peers to generate a unique meme relevant to their understanding and use of select terminology. For instance, students can generate a meme in a synchronous class session, or asynchronously to be shared at a later time or on the class learning management platform or word wall. The meme should contain a popular image or trend, along with class-appropriate text that demonstrates the students' current understanding of the selected term.

Chapter Five

Questioning

As readers, we ask questions. We want to understand what is happening in a story, why it is happening, and what might happen as a result of an event. We question as we read to stimulate our thinking about a concept or topic in order to develop a deeper understanding. Because adolescence is a time when new ideas are being formed, asking students questions provides an opportunity for them to discover what they think. It allows them to explore topics and argue points of view. It presents opportunities for students to interact, as questioning can create spaces for meaningful conversations that involve everyone (Burke, 2010; Christenbury, 2006).

In these conversations, we create ways to critically examine our own connection to and understanding, experience, and analysis of a text. Questioning helps us think beyond the scope of rote understanding, and opens space for critical consideration of personal, social, and universal themes and implications. It encourages the reader to press beyond the status quo, to question the intent, purpose, and effect of the text in one's view and understanding of the world. While we may begin with a focus on questions that promote basic comprehension of the text, our goal as educators is to foster analytic questioning that encourages our students as critical consumers of the world.

Because "what gets asked is what gets considered" (Burke, 2010, p. 259), the types of questions we pose to our students shape what we teach, and how. In the traditional classroom, most teachers scaffold their questioning through the framework of Bloom's taxonomy or Webb's Depth of Knowledge framework. These frameworks move students from recall of factual knowledge to a deeper understanding of a text via analysis, evaluation, synthesis, and extended thinking. We see this in action when a teacher poses a question, students respond, and the teacher asks follow-up questions that move students through these levels. But what does this look like in the online classroom? How can virtual teachers move students toward deeper understanding through questioning?

One major concern regarding questioning in online classrooms can be a lack of student-to-student and student-to-teacher interaction. Virtual teachers can implement questioning strategies in a way that leads to an increase in interaction between students, and between student and teacher, while moving students forward in their thinking. While the types of questions virtual teachers pose to students will remain the same (draw on levels of questions), the approach to questioning will be different. What follows are commonly used questioning strategies and suggestions for how to use these in both synchronous and asynchronous online contexts.

STRATEGIES FOR QUESTIONING IN THE VIRTUAL CLASSROOM

Reciprocal Questioning

Nearly every student has experienced the commonly practiced form of questioning in the classroom—teacher poses a question, student responds, teacher moves on to a new question. But teachers do not need to be the only participants asking questions. Students can also take on the role of "questioner" by crafting a list of questions for the teacher to answer. This strategy is known as reciprocal questioning, or ReQuest. Through this strategy, the roles of teacher and student are shifted in a way that helps to deepen student comprehension. First, in order for students to craft questions for the teacher to answer, they must thoroughly analyze the text (a higher-order skill); through their answers, the teacher reinforces learning.

While the steps to the strategy are simple—students and teacher read a text (or an assigned section of a text), both students and teacher create questions to ask the other, questions are asked, teacher or student answers—we suggest that in order to ensure students are moving forward in their thinking and understanding, the questions progress toward higher-order thinking. In other words, teachers and students should be asking less factual questions and more open-ended questions that require analysis, evaluation, and/or the synthesizing of information. While teachers will have a command of creating these types of questions, students may need some guidance. In order to assist students in this process, the virtual teacher could provide a list of question stems for each level of questioning (see figure 5.1).

The ReQuest strategy is easily implemented in both synchronous and asynchronous formats. In a synchronous format, teachers and students can meet face-to-face virtually, simulating the traditional classroom practice. In this format, the teacher can "see" the students answer the questions and the students can in turn "see" the teacher answer the questions. In this setting, all

Level of Question	Possible Question Stems
Knowledge/Recall • recalling facts, terms, and basic concepts	• Who was . . . ? • What happened after....? • What does ____ mean? • How many ____?
Comprehension • demonstrating understanding of facts and ideas by organizing, comparing, translating, interpreting, giving descriptions and stating main ideas.	• Explain what is meant by ____? • In what ways is ____ like ____? • What is the main idea of ____?
Application • applying acquired knowledge and facts in a different way	• What would result if . . . ? • How would you solve ____ using what you have learned? • What factors would you change if ____? • Why is ____ significant? • How is ____ an example of ____?
Analysis • Examining and breaking information into parts by identifying motives or causes. • Making inferences and finding evidence to support generalizations.	• In what ways is ____ related to ____? • What is the theme of ____? • What is the relationship between ____ and ____? • Outline/diagram/map ____. • Classify ____ according to ____.
Synthesis • Compiling information together in a different way by combining elements in a new pattern or proposing alternative solutions.	• In what ways could you change (modify) the plot (plan) ? • How would you improve ____? • Predict the outcome if ____? • What solutions would you suggest for ____?
Evaluation • Presenting and defending opinions by making judgments about information, validity of ideas or quality of work based on a set of criteria.	• How would you evaluate ____? • What criteria would you use to assess ____? • What changes to ____ would you recommend and why? • What do you think about ____? Support your opinion.

Figure 5.1. Question levels and sample question stems. *Adapted from bloomstaxonomy.org*

students have an opportunity to hear the teacher's questions and each other's questions in real time.

While the strategy calls for teacher-to-student and student-to-teacher questioning, virtual teachers can also ask that students pose their questions to their classmates. Virtual teachers can team students and place each team in a breakout room. Through each approach, virtual teachers can differentiate instruction by requiring each team to craft and pose different levels of questions. For example, if particular students need more practice in demonstrating the understanding of ideas, the teacher can require this team to create comprehension questions.

In an asynchronous format, the virtual teacher and students can post their questions in a class-wide discussion board. Through this format, online learners have open access to the questions and answers, and can use the posts as a tool to prepare for demonstration of mastery.

For example, in a math class, a teacher might post an equation and ask the students how they would solve the problem using what they learned (application). The students would respond with the solution, each step written out in detail. The teacher could ask a follow-up question, asking the students why they performed a particular step (evaluation). Each student could be given the same equation or a separate equation and asked to complete the same task (differentiation). In turn, students could each pose their own equation for the teacher to solve and ask the teacher why they performed a particular step. By making the discussion board responses public, students will be privy to several examples of the approach being used to solve an equation. Additionally, teachers can use student responses as a formative assessment, gauging the students' understanding of how to solve an equation and determining what level of question to pose as a follow-up.

Discussion Directors

Another questioning strategy that shifts the role of teacher and student is the discussion director in a literature circle. Literature circles are a classic and continued trend for small-group book/text discussions (Daniels, 2002). In serving as "discussion directors," students consider thought-provoking, discussion-based questions based on their understanding and reading of the text. Just as students in the traditional classroom can construct questions to engage their peers in a conversation on a story, online students can also learn effective ways to consider, develop, and implement discussion-based questions to encourage social discussion and collaborative learning regarding a course story or novel.

The key to effectively transferring consideration of a discussion director role to the virtual space is ensuring time to explicitly teach readers how to identify and format critical questions, while also providing opportunity for synchronous or asynchronous discussion. To begin, model your own critical questioning for your online students. You can create a video tutorial that guides students through the reading and questioning process, craft a questioning module for students to review on an independent basis, or engage learners in synchronous instruction during which you discuss and practice your approach to crafting critical questions.

The goal is to provide modeled instruction to students so that they understand the difference between basic, comprehension-based questions, or yes/no questioning structure, and questions that provoke connection, thought, and open-discussion of key concepts and themes within the text. Instead of questions that rely strictly on memorization of facts from the story, encourage students to think deeper by crafting questions that push beyond the text toward more universal or societal implications.

Once students have the opportunity to learn more about the goals and structure of strong, critical questions, it is time to engage learners in their own development and student-led discussions of the text. If you have the opportunity to engage learners in synchronous discussion, structure the online lesson in a way that promotes student voice, allowing students to first share in a small group or partner setting before moving towards a whole-class discussion, and encourage your students to respond and reference the text when possible. The objective is to encourage critical consideration of the text, self, and world through collaborative learning and social interaction.

If you do not have the opportunity to engage students in a synchronous discussion of the course material, you can still utilize discussion director roles with a variety of video or text-based applications. Students can record an initial video in which they share out their questions about the story. Classmates can then log in, respond with their own video or text reply, and come back later to view the ideas shared out by fellow readers. While the asynchronous method of conversation may not have the same direct impact as a more immediate discussion, students still have an opportunity to question, consider, and collaborate on their critical reading and interpretation of the text.

Question the Author

The types of texts that students read vary by content area. For example, in an English language arts (ELA) class, students read fiction and nonfiction in several formats (e.g., poetry, memoirs, letters, short stories). In a history class, students read both primary (e.g., speeches, letters, newspapers) and secondary sources. In a science course, students do a lot of technical reading (e.g., lab reports, research articles). But no matter the content area, students explore a text's message, intent, and claim(s). One strategy that teachers can implement when analyzing and evaluating these characteristics is "Question the Author," or QtA (McKeown et al., 1997).

According to Fisher and Frey (2016), the QtA strategy "asks students to pose queries *while* reading a given text, helping to solidify their knowledge and challenge their understanding, rather than *after* reading" (p. 17). In doing so, this strategy engages students with the text in an interpretive manner that requires them to create deeper meaning by critiquing the authors' writing (Simon, 2015). The questions that students seek to answer using this strategy are:

- What is the author saying? (Cite evidence from the text to support your response.)

- Why is the author telling you that?
- Is it stated clearly? If not, how might the author have stated it more clearly?
- What might you have said instead? (adapted from Jones, 2012).

In the traditional classroom, the teacher has an opportunity to either read aloud, stopping at specific points in the text to pose these questions, or have students read a section individually and then pose questions to engage learners in meaningful discussion. In a virtual classroom, where students are separated by time and space, this questioning strategy may seem impossible to implement. However, there are several approaches a virtual teacher can use when utilizing the QtA strategy.

First, online teachers could ask students to provide written responses. The teacher can create and share a graphic organizer that contains stopping points within the reading. At each stopping point, the teacher can ask students to answer the questions posed above. This graphic organizer can be housed in a shared file so the teacher can monitor each student's understanding as they read through each assigned section. In approaching the strategy in this way, the teacher has the opportunity to offer feedback during the reading process.

Virtual teachers can also utilize verbal or visual mediums to implement this instructional strategy. Teachers can record themselves reading a section of text using a tool such as VoiceThread, or visually through an application such as Flipgrid. At the end of the reading, the virtual teacher can pose the above questions and ask students to respond verbally or visually using the same application. Students can send their verbal responses directly to the teacher and the teacher can reply to the student via verbal or visual response. The teacher repeats this process until the entire text is read. This format emulates a dialogic discussion, similar to those practiced in the traditional classroom.

While the approaches described above focus on the individual student completing the task, virtual teachers can also implement this strategy with small teams, or as a whole class activity. Teachers can create breakout rooms for teams of students and each team can work together to answer the questions after each indicated stopping point in the text. Students can work asynchronously through Google Docs, each recording their response in a different color font, or synchronously, all meeting at the same time and answering the questions together. If virtual teachers have students meeting synchronously to participate in this strategy, they can opt to join the discussion or allow the discussion to be student-led and student-centered.

Chapter Six

Online Classroom Conversation and Collaboration

As teachers of literacy, we understand that learning does not exist in a vacuum. As we collaborate with others, we have the opportunity to expand our own connections, considerations, and understandings of the world. As we engage students in reading and writing, we want to provide opportunities to share and learn from one another. We want to give students the chance to have their assumptions challenged, to perceive texts in new ways, and to share their voices in a space that values their experience and insight. For this reason, it is essential we identify means of engaging online learners in conversation and collaboration within the virtual setting.

Reading is a social process, anchored in social constructivism. What this perspective purports is that learning develops and deepens with interaction between learners (Romiszowski & Mason, 2004). As such, it is important that virtual teachers include opportunities for online students to collaborate and discuss what they read. As McElhone (2014) shared, discussion "is a crucial tool for comprehending, learning from, synthesizing across, and generating new ideas with texts" (p. 2). The online environment lends itself well to the social constructivist perspective of learning, as computer-mediated communication tools such as emails, discussion boards and conferencing applications, and collaborative platforms such as Zoom, VoiceThread, and Voki make it possible for discussions and collaboration to occur in both asynchronous and synchronous contexts.

Through the implementation of discussion and collaboration tasks in the virtual classroom, online learners can show what they know and talk out ideas in ways similar to those experienced in traditional classrooms, which can transform and deepen their thinking (McElhone, 2014). However, it takes preparation on the teacher's part and practice on the students' part.

Research informs us that when students are asked to engage in conversations around academic tasks without preparation, expectations, and ground rules, conversations stray and often fail to delve deep into academic content (McElhone, 2014; Mercer & Littleton, 2007; Nichols, 2008).

Classrooms should be safe places for students to explore and share their thoughts and ideas without the threat of hostile or inappropriate responses. Because questioning and collaboration can ask students to take a risk in sharing their beliefs, attitudes, and perceptions, prior to implementing any of the strategies presented in this chapter, a virtual teacher should set collaboration and discussion expectations and ground rules.

STRATEGIES FOR ENGAGING VIRTUAL LEARNERS IN ASYNCHRONOUS COLLABORATION

The very nature of online learning often leads to asynchronous communication. While teachers may not always be able to engage in real-time collaboration with students, the key is identifying effective means of encouraging collaboration among our online learners. After all, learning occurs in a social space. The more creative teachers are in approaching asynchronous collaboration through multiple channels and applications, the more likely you can connect and engage even the most reluctant of online learners. The key is promoting authentic, enriching asynchronous collaboration. You want students to really share and learn with and from one another—not simply post and reply for the sake of a grade or course completion.

The following strategies approach asynchronous peer collaboration from three key angles: video, audio, and text exchange. While all formats or approaches may not be accessible or effective for every virtual learning endeavor or student, we are hopeful that the strategies can serve as a starting point in identifying the exchange approach and applications that best serve your course and student needs.

Video Exchange

The first approach to asynchronous collaboration speaks to visual and auditory connection. Social presence is key to connecting and engaging students within an asynchronous platform. What better way to establish such presence than through applications that promote the sharing of student faces and voices? As students are able to log in and see and hear their classmates, they are able to connect faces to the course assignment, discussion, and collaborative learning.

There are a plethora of online websites and applications that promote asynchronous video connection among online learners. Such sites enable students to record and share videos that promote the sharing of ideas, questions, and insights. It is important to identify websites or applications that are easy to navigate for the purpose of the course. In addition, it is a good idea to incorporate privacy settings that limit sharing and public access. For example, a current application that lends itself to encouraging student engagement and collaboration is Flipgrid.

Flipgrid is a free, online program for educators that promotes the sharing of one- to five-minute student and teacher videos. Teachers create course "grids" that contain guiding directives and videos. Teachers can lock grids so that students are required to log in through a password-secured site. Or, teachers can limit access strictly to students by incorporating a class roster and providing individual access codes to log in to the class grid. Teachers can create multiple threads within a single class grid as a means of encouraging response to multiple prompts, or to encourage small-group discussions. Students simply log in to their class grid, locate their small-group thread, view posted videos, and respond! Student responses can take the form of an emoji response to a posted video or a reply video post.

Flipgrid offers a lot of opportunities for teachers to navigate online video collaborations while maintaining oversight and ease of assessment. Teachers can post grading feedback for students within the online application. They can also see a record of student views, posts, replies, and responses. In addition, teachers can opt to regulate posts by requiring educator approval for posting and viewing. This means teachers can view student videos before they are shared and viewed by other students. Such features offer online teachers the opportunity to connect, engage, and assess learners throughout their engagement with the asynchronous video platform.

While Flipgrid is just one of many online video-hosting websites, the key to effective video exchange in seeking student collaboration is access, feasibility, structure, and security. Ensure that the application or website promotes a sense of security for learners as they post their videos to the online system. Students should feel safe in sharing their identity, voice, and work within a virtual platform. In addition, consider cost and accessibility for all online learners. If students find that they must invest more time in understanding how to navigate and utilize a suggested platform, they will be less inclined to invest time in viewing and critically responding to such videos as they are posted and shared by classmates.

With regard to structure, we suggest finding applications or video-hosting sites that provide options in terms of video length and response. If video posts are too lengthy, students may be dissuaded from giving their full attention to student posts and responses. In addition, strive to encourage a bit of fun and active engagement throughout the video production and sharing process. Just as Flipgrid allows students to add stickers, selfies, and emojis, a variety of online platforms and applications can take something seemingly simple, and utilize it to really excite and motivate adolescent learners.

Audio Exchange

If video is not an option, you can still find ways to incorporate student voice within asynchronous collaboration. Even if students can't see the face on the other side of the screen, they can connect and learn from one another through auditory sharing. For example, VoiceThread is a common platform for engaging students in asynchronous conversation through voice response. VoiceThread provides space for teachers and students to post presentations, slides, and documents. Students can view the posted presentation and contribute their ideas by speaking and typing ideas along a continuous thread of collaboration. Online learners can move forward and backward throughout the posted thread, add replies and comments, and proceed through a provided presentation at a speed that works to encourage their individual understanding and collaboration.

Teachers can utilize platforms such as VoiceThread to share information with students in a presentation format that is interactive and conversational despite the asynchronous nature of the virtual tool. Again, it is important to identify an audio platform that students can access and navigate with relative ease and security. Programs that provide some form of visual component to accompany the audio piece, such as VoiceThread's ability to share presentations and documents, can provide an additional layer of collaboration that works to actively engage and connect learners across time and space.

Text Exchange

Finally, it's important to also remember the value of text or written word in producing peer-to-peer collaboration and learning. Discussion boards have long been implemented as a key means of encouraging asynchronous discussion. However, such posts also risk contributing more to student compliance than they do active collaboration and learning. The key is engagement—not compliance. With so many applications, social media platforms, and programs at our fingertips, why not take full advantage of the opportunity to utilize such programs for student collaboration and development?

Social media can be a force of good, if we find ways to effectively utilize it within our online learning activities. A variety of platforms offer opportunities for students to post, respond, and share with one another. As virtual educators, we can create social media pages or identities that we utilize specifically for the purpose of encouraging asynchronous collaboration within our online course. For example, a course page on Facebook, Twitter, Instagram, or TikTok can be used to post book recommendations, character descriptions, critical discussion questions, and so much more! The key is taking the time to monitor the course page and facilitating respectful, critical discussion among learners. Some platforms provide greater opportunity for private sharing of information than others.

Teachers can also utilize applications to encourage student collaboration and discussion. For instance, Voxer is a current app utilized by teachers and students alike to engage in small-group conversation. This free application, when downloaded to one's phone, tablet, or computer, can engage participants through the sharing of text messages, audio messages, GIF files, photos, and more! Teachers can simply create a unique "Voxer Chatroom" for their class. Students are invited to join the group chat and create a unique name and photo for their program profile. Students and teachers can then exchange messages with one another to create an ongoing, asynchronous conversation surrounding a topic of interest. The program provides the option for alerting users to new posts through notifications. While there is the option of sending one-on-one private messages through the application, teachers can work with students and families to discuss the role and purpose of the application in maintaining focus on coursework and collaborative learning.

OVERCOMING CHALLENGES TO ASYNCHRONOUS COLLABORATION

As online educators, your goal is to actively engage learners in collaboration through asynchronous channels. Yet, reality dictates there are distinct limitations to our ability to effectively reach and teach adolescents in a collaborative manner within an asynchronous environment. Teachers must identify the potential challenges to such collaboration, and search for measures they can put into place that will limit the impact of such challenges for students.

Hello? Who Is This?

While text exchange is a viable option for asynchronous collaboration, it is important to remember that within this form of connection you cannot "see" or "hear" the voice on the other end of the screen. Teachers and students are limited in knowing who is sharing and responding to questions and ideas along the way. While you aim to maintain trust that students are fully engaging and sharing their own ideas, thoughts, and words, teachers inevitably need to maintain checkpoints as a means of verifying academic integrity and engagement.

One way to counter this potential challenge to asynchronous collaboration is discussion-based reflection and response. Simply take time throughout the week to reach out via visual or auditory platforms to connect and further conversation with students. For example, during a phone call with the student, ask them to elaborate or share more about a recent text exchange or thread. Take time to read through student responses and identify potential areas of academic integrity or redundancy in student collaboration. As you get to know your students, and as you engage with them in both asynchronous and synchronous ways, maintain a record and reflection of student ideas, questions, and contributions. If something feels "off," take time to consider how you might best approach the situation to ensure students are authentically engaging and sharing with one another within the asynchronous platform.

Missing in Action

Asynchronous collaboration requires moments of critical, active engagement. But, what can teachers do when you set the stage for collaboration, only to discover students are either not contributing, or appear to be contributing just enough to meet course requirements? As we have previously noted, motivation is key to online learning engagement. Revisit chapter 2 and see if you can identify ways of reaching out and building on your relationship and connection with students and families to encourage more asynchronous engagement. Let the students know you are present—that you are fully invested in encouraging their active collaboration and that you are aware of their presence, or lack of engagement, within the class dialogue. And, take time to help them understand the purpose of the interaction and role they are expected to serve in leading, facilitating, participating in, and encouraging others throughout the collaborative process. No one step or course of action will meet the needs of all learners. As you grow to know your students and cultivate solid relationships with learners, identify the methods and approaches that work best to further engagement and productivity within the asynchronous collaborative environment.

STRATEGIES FOR ENGAGING VIRTUAL LEARNERS IN SYNCHRONOUS COLLABORATION

If provided the option or opportunity, synchronous engagement is the way to go in terms of fully immersing online learners in peer-to-peer collaboration. Nothing beats in-the-moment conversation. The traditional classroom provides teachers with rich pedagogical tools for actively engaging students in critical reading and discussion of texts. In this section, we hope to assist you in translating some of the more prominent means of traditional classroom reading discussion to the synchronous virtual setting. How can we take what we know works, and shape it for this new classroom context?

Whole-Class Synchronous Collaboration

Learning management systems (LMS) provide today's online teachers with the virtual space to conduct synchronous instruction. Each system provides tools and opportunity for teacher-to-student, as well as student-to-student interaction unique to the application. For example, Blackboard is an LMS that infuses a variety of tools and a virtual whiteboard for live instruction, discussion threads, classroom modules, online assessment, and more. As you train and learn more about the LMS utilized within your online classroom, identify ways you can adapt your traditional classroom pedagogy to fit the confines of this new context.

For instance, in the traditional classroom setting, many ELA teachers utilize whole-class reading or novel discussion during direct instruction. But, how might a virtual teacher implement a similar practice within the online setting? Applications such as Blackboard provide teachers with a real-time virtual "classroom." Students log in to the online class session through their computer, tablet, or phone at a predetermined date and time. The teacher can take on the role of "moderator," operating the virtual whiteboard, sharing a computer screen, playing videos, messaging students through the text feature, and maintaining control of the classroom microphone and video options. The teacher can have students log in as "participants" who have the ability to also share via video, microphone, text, or whiteboard application. The class can follow along with a provided text displayed on the classroom whiteboard, respond to questions using their built-in microphones, and contribute ideas through the text message app or by typing onto the whiteboard screen.

Small-Group Synchronous Collaboration

Teachers within the traditional classroom also utilize small, collaborative group activities when engaging students in reading collaboration and conversation. Virtual teachers can accomplish the same objectives within the synchronous online platform. Learning management systems and online applications, such as Zoom Meeting, provide space for teachers to transition students from a whole-class conversation toward a small-group discussion. Virtual breakout rooms, such as those provided within the Blackboard LMS, provide a space within a larger synchronous platform for small-group conversation. For instance, teachers can create a distinct number of breakout rooms within their online classroom space, and virtually "move" students into rooms in either a random or predetermined manner.

Teachers can set up the breakout rooms in advance so that they contain unique directions, questions, texts, videos, and other resources within each room. Once students are relocated from the whole-class space into the smaller breakout rooms, the teacher can pop in and out of select rooms as a means of checking in on student conversation and progress. Students within each room can have access to a variety of tools to assist them in carrying out the small-group tasks or directives as a collaborative group. Teachers can set timers to help keep students on track and progressing through the designated reading tasks. Once the time has expired, teachers can either allow additional time for students to continue working, or move all learners back to the communal space to share their progress and work with the entire class.

Much like the traditional classroom, this approach to small-group instruction offers learners a chance to actively engage with one another in meaningful ways, with teacher scaffolding and support as needed. In addition, it provides a way for groups to then share out their work and discussion with the entire class, much like whole-class discussion and reflection at the end of the day's lesson within the traditional classroom setting.

OVERCOMING CHALLENGES TO SYNCHRONOUS COLLABORATION

Every classroom contains a wide array of potential challenges or hazards to student collaboration and discussion. The same can be said for synchronous instruction within the virtual space. It is important to identify potential hazards, and plan for ways to overcome such obstacles to ensure student engagement and meaningful collaboration.

Technical Difficulties

Technology can be both a blessing and a curse. In the traditional classroom, teachers prepare for potential technological difficulties when planning and executing daily instruction. In the virtual setting, our students will encounter technological difficulties that are beyond our ability to navigate or control in the moment. Such difficulties may lead to a student missing out on vital synchronous instruction or collaboration. For this reason, it can be important to ensure your ability to record synchronous instruction and provide access to the recording for your students.

While we know that viewing a recording of instruction is not as valuable or effective in promoting active collaboration as in-the-moment engagement, providing students access to information they might otherwise miss due to a technological absence can be crucial to ensuring their progress and success within the course. If a student seems to have technological difficulties with great frequency, be sure to reach out to the student and family. See what might be causing the difficulty, and how you can offer assistance to allow your student to navigate the synchronous platform with ease and fluidity.

In addition to recording synchronous lessons, try to find ways to harness multiple avenues of, or channels for, connection for your students. For example, if a student has difficulty logging into the synchronous session via a computer or tablet, see if there might be a way they can join the conversation through their phone or handheld device. A lot of online applications and LMS platforms offer a dial-in option for participants. While a dial-in option may not provide the same level of collaboration or engagement as a more visual application, this option can still provide students the opportunity to listen, speak, and engage with peers in the discussion.

Finally, always prepare for the unexpected. In the traditional classroom, teachers work around sudden fire drills, assemblies, schedule changes, and classroom interruptions. It is just as important to plan ahead and consider the many ways technology might play a role in interrupting intended goals for a synchronous session. What should students do if the teacher is suddenly logged out of the online session? How might students get assistance if they cannot access the synchronous classroom space? What alternatives are in place for online tools that might fail to work or be as effective as once intended? Just as you prepare for the unexpected and roll with the punches in the traditional setting, it is important to plan ahead and identify ways you can overcome technological challenges as they come into play during your synchronous instruction.

Encouraging All Voices

In any class discussion, whether it be in a traditional classroom or an online setting, there is the chance that some students will speak up and speak out, while others may remain more withdrawn or passive in their choice to share and collaborate. The key to any collaboration is identifying ways to elevate all voices, experiences, and identities within the classroom. Virtual teachers can adapt a lot of what they practice in the traditional space, and mold it to work within the synchronous online platform to encourage student participation and sharing.

The use of breakout rooms, as mentioned previously, is an important way to encourage conversation within small groups and to adapt proximity control for the online classroom. Students who may not feel safe or comfortable speaking up within a whole-class setting might feel more inclined to share and connect within a small-group discussion. Moving students into smaller, more personable spaces can help support those who may not be as inclined to speak up when navigating a larger virtual classroom context. In addition, the ability to move freely from one group to another provides teachers the opportunity to check in with students, provide a sense of proximity to the discussion, and encourage on-task discussion and collaboration in what might otherwise be a distant or secluded space.

In the traditional classroom, teachers may use worksheets or graphic organizers to help students navigate the flow of conversation, engage in collaborative learning, and maintain focus on the day's content objective. Online templates or graphic organizers can accomplish the same goals within the virtual classroom. Many LMS tools provide teachers the means to share files with students or post such templates to the virtual whiteboard. Students can examine, collaborate, and complete such handouts in real time while participating in whole-class or small-group reading and discussion. Referencing shared files or virtual whiteboards can provide the same level of engagement and collaboration as within the traditional classroom space. Such templates or organizers can provide necessary differentiation and scaffolding for learners as a means of encouraging all students to participate and learn in a way that meets their instructional needs and elevates their voice and unique experience.

Another way virtual teachers can encourage active collaboration for all students is through the assigning of student roles and responsibilities during whole-class or small-group engagement. Just as teachers in the traditional space often identify and assign students key responsibilities or tasks for lessons and activities, virtual teachers can utilize similar roles for online learning and collaboration. For instance, a student can take on the role of discussion director and assume responsibility for initiating small-group discussion and conversation. Or, a student can assume the role of note-taker and make note of student ideas and questions on the virtual whiteboard. Another student may fulfill the role of researcher and share websites, videos, or images from an online search related to the conversation at hand. Finding unique ways for students to assume a level of individual responsibility to the group or class endeavor is an effective way of promoting active engagement within a synchronous class discussion or activity. It allows students to build on personal strengths or talents, contribute within the social learning context, and find value in their efforts toward collaboration.

Preparation prior to a synchronous class session is just as important for the students as it is for the teacher. It is not uncommon for traditional classroom instruction to include student homework or tasks prior to engaging in collaborative learning or conversation. The same is true for virtual learning. Ask students to come to the synchronous session prepared to engage and share out with their classmates. Such preparation may mean that students read preselected material, complete a set of mathematical computations before the class meets, examine or construct a set of discussion questions, or perhaps conduct independent research prior to the class session. Student preparation can go a long way in maintaining a focus, flow, and critical conversation surrounding course texts and material. The more prepared students are to engage in conversation and collaboration, the more prepared they will be to actively listen and learn from the myriad of voices in the online classroom.

Finally, find ways to maintain active insight regarding students who are more apprehensive, disconnected, or disengaged from class collaboration. Teachers can maintain personal notes or checklists of student participation throughout the whole-class or small-group synchronous session. Don't hesitate to simply check in with learners during discussions and activities. You might send the student a private chat message or text.

A quick "Hey! How are things? You following along okay?" can offer a great deal of insight into student activity, presence, or understanding without risk of embarrassment in the social space. Some programs notify the teacher when the student is no longer active within the virtual classroom. Try to keep track of student presence, and reach out as necessary. If you notice a student is frequently away from the computer, or seems to disconnect from discussion, take advantage of different avenues of communication to verify the student is on track, learning, listening, and motivated to engage in the classroom activity.

Chapter Seven

Engaging Critical Literacies in the Online Classroom

Reading can serve as an act of empowerment. Not only does it provide an opportunity to reflect on our own experience and identity, but it provides a glimpse into the myriad of contexts and lives outside our niche in the world. The key is pushing beyond a singular acceptance and understanding of a text toward a critical examination that promotes reflection, questions, and challenges. We want to encourage students to do more than engage with a story. We want to empower them as critical consumers in interpretations that identify hidden bias, expose false claims, question perspective, and seek out that which is privileged and that which is silenced.

Perhaps now more than any other time in history, students need to become critical consumers of texts as they learn to navigate a world that is not only changing at a rapid pace, but one that is becoming more complex (Moje et al., 2000). Therefore, "rather than offer more reading strategy instruction, teachers must offer a different kind of instruction—instruction that defines reading strategies as a set of resources for exploring both written texts and the texts of students' lived realities" (Park, 2012, p. 630).

There are two tenets of critical literacy that all teachers need to acknowledge. The first is that "reading is not a set of free-floating skills, independent of social contexts and devoid of ideologies" (Park, 2012, p. 631), and the second is that texts are socially constructed. Through a critical literacy lens, readers utilize texts as a means of seeking out, understanding, and taking action against matters of injustice and inequity in the world. Readers come to question the power dynamics within society that generate what we often consider to be the norm, as presented in texts. Through this approach to reading, "texts can be deconstructed and reconstructed for the purpose of changing problematic ways of being or doing" (Vasquez & Felderman, 2012, p. 5).

STRATEGIES FOR ENGAGING VIRTUAL LEARNERS IN CRITICAL LITERACIES

Text Selection

While many curricula maintain emphasis on the canon, the ever-growing body of diverse middle-level and young adult literature provides a world of opportunity for the online classroom. The first step in encouraging critical literacy is the selection of texts. Ideally, you want to allow readers to engage in texts that promote consideration of a diverse array of cultures, lives, and experiences and diverse ways of being in the world. A trend towards "own voices" texts, or texts written by individuals who identify as a member of the marginalized community on which they focus within the narrative, is a movement that emphasizes the importance of voice and lived experience. Such texts provide readers insight into experiences that speak from a place of critical understanding. In selecting such works, the teacher can further encourage students to reflect on their own experiences, strive to connect with diverse identities, and consider ways of viewing society that may extend beyond the accepted "norm."

Virtual teachers can begin the search for own voices narratives through online search engines or social media outlets that promote the sharing and distribution of such titles. For example, Twitter provides hashtags such as #OwnVoices and #DisruptTexts that are utilized by educators, authors, and others to share text suggestions, resources, and thoughts to consider when engaging in diverse texts. In selecting texts for the classroom, consider how you might embrace a broader diversity of titles and experiences within the curriculum. Common threads provide a simple and effective way of exploring potential titles, authors, and themes of focus for classroom texts.

In addition to the consideration of own voices titles, consider engaging readers in texts that embrace a wide array of lived experiences and voices. Think beyond a singular definition of "diversity" and consider how you can push students to critically question assumptions about a "normalized" sense of identity or way of being. For example, seek out titles that reflect diversity with regard to race, ethnicity, and culture, as well as neurological and body diversity. Incorporate titles that move beyond the heteronormative, cis-gender character development towards more queer-inclusive works. Again, virtual search engines and social media websites offer virtual teachers a world of titles and book reviews for quick and careful textual identification and consideration.

In the event you are unable to expand reading selections beyond a prescribed curriculum or content selection, consider ways to encourage students to engage in independent text selections that embrace a diverse array of authors, characters, experiences, and genres. By utilizing methods noted in previous chapters for text selection and sharing, students can engage in independent selection and reading activities that encourage critical literacy outside of the whole-class or small-group novel selections.

Critical Text Analysis and Note-Taking

Once you have identified novels, primary or secondary sources, textbooks, and other materials for the classroom, it's important to encourage students as critical consumers. You want students to consider and navigate each text in a way that allows them to identify how their own lens, experience, and understanding of the world speaks to their interpretation of the content. You want students to question their understanding of the text, the position of the author, and power dynamics within their interpretations.

There are many different approaches to taking notes. Some students prefer to take notes using framed formats (outlines, two-column notes), while others prefer to be more creative and draft visual notes (mind maps, sketchnotes). No matter the preference, Nwokoreze (1990) suggests that "it is during the note-taking stage that students reach the highest level of comprehension" (p. 42), making note-taking an important process during reading to develop comprehension (Marzano et al., 2001).

Just as in the traditional classroom, readers in an online class can benefit from a variety of note-taking strategies that will help them identify critical elements and consider their interpretations of a text as they read through a critical lens. Teachers can utilize online note-taking applications, shared online documents, and interactive graphic organizers to engage learners in the note-taking process.

Cornell Notes

Created by Walter Pauk in 1954, Cornell Notes is a note-taking strategy that asks students to record detailed information from the text as they read, listing any questions, main ideas, or vocabulary words that arise from the reading, and summarize what they read. All this information is recorded on a one-page graphic organizer divided into three sections: Notes, Cues, and Summary (see figure 7.1).

In the "Notes" section, students actively take notes while they read. While most students will want to write out their notes in complete sentences, often citing the text directly, suggest to them that their notes can be completed with bullet points, abbreviations, or symbols. In doing so, students can save space

Figure 7.1. Sample Cornell Notes template. *Created by the authors*

in recording the critical elements presented within the text, allowing for more details to be included.

The "Cues" section is completed after students have read and taken notes. Here, students record any questions about the reading they have, any main ideas that are presented in the reading, and record any vocabulary words that were defined in the text. If the virtual teacher wants students to note specific critical elements as they read, students can be reminded to do so in the "Cues" section. For example, the teacher could pose questions that guide students on what to notate during reading in order to help students determine what information is most important, or even ask students to make text-to-self connections.

At the bottom of the graphic organizer, students are prompted to summarize what they have read. Before students write their summary, it is important to direct them to review their notes and cues, especially if the teacher has provided prompts and questions in the "Cues" section.

While Cornell Notes graphic organizers are commonly organized in the format described above, there are several websites that offer teachers free access to create individual or unique versions of this graphic organizer. For example, Wufoo allows teachers to create individualized, or content-specific Cornell Notes graphic organizers.

Virtual teachers can provide students with a Cornell Notes graphic organizer in several ways. First, they can email students the graphic organizer as a Word document, or post the Word document in the materials section of the course for students to download. Students could be asked to type directly into the graphic organizer, or they can print it and take notes by hand, then upload the completed graphic organizer to the course assignment tab or email it directly to the teacher.

If the virtual teacher wants to monitor students' comprehension as they work through a section of text, the other option could be to create a graphic organizer as a Google Doc and share it with each student. Through this approach both teacher and students have access, and teachers can monitor comprehension as students read, offering feedback in the form of comments if students need redirection or guidance.

Mind Maps

While handwritten or typed notes are the most commonly practiced form of note-taking, they have some limitations. First, these forms of notes tend to be linear. While this is great for some content areas, for others it might not work well. Using graphic organizers to take notes can limit the amount of information that a student can record. Additionally, taking handwritten or typed notes can become monotonous and boring. And lastly, students often tend to write or type notes verbatim. In an effort to encourage creativity in the classroom while still asking students to take notes as they read, another note-taking strategy that can be beneficial to online students is mind maps. Mind maps provide an opportunity for students to record important information in a nonlinear, visual format.

Created on a blank page, students begin by writing (or typing) the subject or topic in the center of the page. From there, students add branches that extend out, each branch attached to a specific note (see figure 7.2). For virtual students, the two-dimensional structure of this note-taking strategy encourages the use of images, colors, and even links in their notes, which can help students remember concepts and topics better. With mind maps, students also have the ability to go back and add additional notes, as space is less of an issue than with traditional linear note-taking formats. Overall, as students work through this strategy, they are active in creating notes instead of transcribing them.

One strength of using mind maps as a note-taking strategy is that it can be done individually or in teams. Students can begin by creating their mind map individually as a way for the virtual teacher to gauge comprehension. Once completed, students can share their maps in teams or with the whole class. Asynchronously, teachers can post all student mind maps in a shared class folder or on a discussion board so all students are able to view their peers' maps. Students could be asked to view a specific number of classmates' maps and respond to them in writing. Virtual teachers could also assign students to teams, where they share their maps with their teammates in a private discussion group. Virtual teachers can arrange for all students to meet synchronously via Zoom or Skype to share their maps, or students can be assigned to a team and each team meets virtually to share.

While virtual students can create mind maps independent of a graphic organizer, there are several free applications they can utilize to guide them in their note creations. Miro, Draw.io, Coggle, XMind, and MindMeister are just a few free mind map resources available.

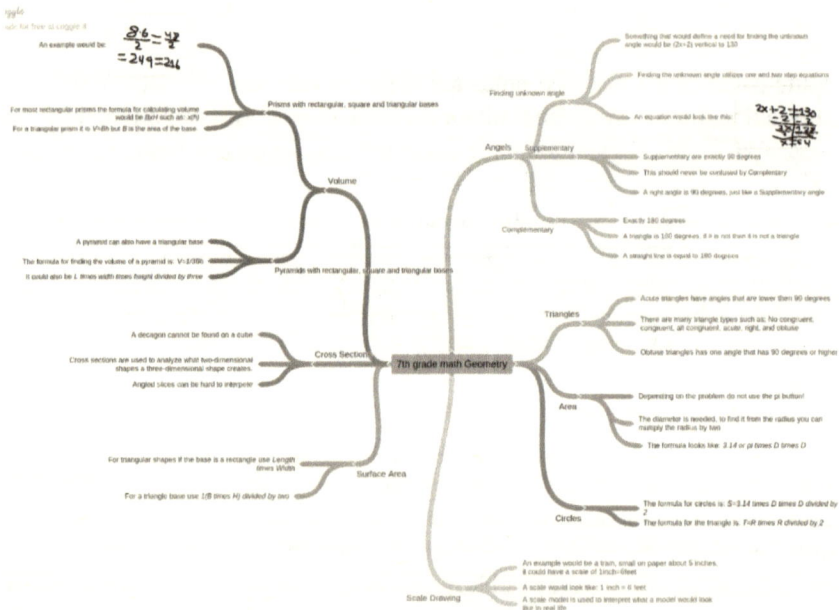

Figure 7.2. Sample geometry mind map. *Courtesy of Coggle*

Online Literature Circles

In chapter 5, we introduced the idea of transferring the literature circle role of discussion director to the virtual classroom space. In addition to this singular role, online learners can implement and engage in literature circle discussions in a manner similar to the traditional classroom environment. Roles such as "vocabulary enricher," "literary luminary," "researcher," and more (Daniels, 2002) can be adapted so that students collaborate in critical engagement with the text in either an asynchronous or synchronous fashion. The important thing to remember when infusing a focus on critical literacy with literature circle engagement is to center student attention on using a critical lens to engage with the text and in their discussions with one another.

For instance, as students identify vocabulary they deem to be essential to the text, ask that they also consider why particular terminology is utilized in crafting and sharing the story. Why might the author have elected to incorporate particular vocabulary terms, dialect, cultural references, and more? How might such vocabulary speak to the character's privilege or that of marginalized or silenced voices? With regard to passage selection, how might the literary luminary identify passages that highlight aspects of injustice or power dynamics within the text? Or, how might students carry out additional research with regard to themes of injustice that will later be translated into action projects for positive change?

As students carry out their individual roles and engage in reading of the text, provide an asynchronous or synchronous space for collaboration and thoughtful discussion. Students might record and share videos, reply to videos, and take time to reflect between postings when engaging in asynchronous literature circle groups. If students are able to log in and engage in conversation at a single point in time, you might encourage dialogue through online learning systems such as Blackboard Collaborate, GoToMeeting, or Skype. Conference call applications will allow students to come together, converse, and encourage one another in developing their critical lens and literacy skills.

Beyond Reader Response Journals

Reader response criticism theory promotes active engagement with the text through the cultivation of connections (Rosenblatt, 1978). Popularized in the 1970s, this theory of textual engagement continues to hold prominence in today's classrooms. It views reading as an active transaction between the text and reader. The text does not exist in isolation. Rather, as the reader engages with the text, they construct meaning through connection and schema. Engaging students in critical literacy further encourages them to extend beyond the development and appreciation of connection with characters and story. In utilizing a reader response approach as a starting point, students can then reflect on their connections to consider the assumptions, implications, hidden perspectives/experiences, and silences that exist within their interpretations and understandings of the text.

To begin, identify an online resource to utilize as a platform for student reader response journaling. Students might utilize a class or personal blog site, word processing program, or personalized discussion board platform that provides the space and privacy necessary for students to generate initial ideas and later share as necessary with their classmates and teacher. Students might also annotate and document connections directly in a provided or accessible e-book.

Help students to see the potential for drawing on a variety of connections as they engage with a story. Begin with a clear focus on engaging student schema, or their prior experiences, thoughts, knowledge, emotions and connections. Students might identify text-to-self, text-to-text, or text-to-world connections as they actively read the story. Encourage them to begin simply by sharing and identifying connections as they occur. Then, ask them to read over their connections and identify the structure. Are most connections of a personal nature? Are they identifying a variety of textual connections relevant to other stories, news, or outside sources? Are they finding that their reading of the text aligns with their awareness of society, current events, or key moments in history?

After your readers identify their connections and the structure of said connections, press them toward a state of critical literacy via additional reflection and consideration of each connection. For instance, in reflecting on their text-to-self connections, ask students to consider how their connection speaks to their current state of privilege or position of power in the world. Or, they might consider the ways in which their connection speaks to their own experiences with injustice or marginalization within society. How does the personal connection afford them the opportunity to see a reflection of their own experience, or how might it promote consideration of a voice and experience outside of their own? How does a personal connection leave potential for assumptions and judgment? How might an overabundance of personal connection potentially cloud or influence one's ability to see the unique experiences of the character or narrator in greater depth? In other words, when we fall back on our own experience as a way of filtering our perceptions of another's experience or story, how might we limit our ability to be open and considerate of how the other's experience is different from our own? In addition, if our readers find limited personal connection to the text, what might this mean in terms of their current level of understanding or experience regarding the diversity presented within the story? How might they seek out a deeper level of personal connection and understanding as a way of further engaging with diverse experiences within the text?

For students who identify text-to-text or text-to-world connections, encourage them beyond the initial connection to a critical interpretation of how the story speaks to the voice and experience of others. What do these connections reveal for them in reflecting on their interpretations of society and worldly events? Is there a commonality among the numerous connections they have identified? What might this commonality mean? How might it speak to their identity as a reader and critical consumer of text? What understanding or voice appears to be missing from the connections they have drawn upon throughout their engagement with the story? And, finally, how do all of these connections and considerations speak to their interpretation of the text at hand?

Virtual students can access online applications, websites, and programs that promote deeper reflection and identify connections among initial responses to the text. Students can begin by highlighting, brainstorming, and freewriting their thoughts from the initial connections. They may highlight key words or themes that surface within their connections in a word processing program. In seeking out the commonalities and overarching themes within their initial response, they can strive to question and consider the significance of such commonalities within their reading and interpretations of text. Students can also work with one another in a synchronous or asynchronous manner to read, reply, and question one another's connections as they are posted and shared within a classroom blog or discussion board thread. In working with a partner, students can encourage one another to view their connections and interpretations in a new way. Students can work in a collaborative and respectful way to encourage one another in their critical interpretation and examination of connections to a variety of texts.

From Consumption to Action

The key to critical literacy is extending beyond textual analysis toward action for change. You want to empower learners to move from a state of awareness toward involvement. As virtual teachers, you have the means to provide space for students to do more than read and analyze text. You have access to resources that promote engagement and action for enhancing awareness and positive change. Encourage students to think beyond the text and limitations of the current status quo toward a place of positive change or growth. Then, utilize the resources of virtual learning to help students research, create, direct, and implement a project that builds on their critical literacy and recent textual engagement. However, given the separation in time and space, there are important considerations to be made as you encourage students to move forward in service-based learning or critical actions within their communities.

Research

Virtual learners have a plethora of research at their fingertips. You want to begin by teaching explicit research skills that help students navigate through credible versus misleading websites, news articles, journal articles, and more. Once students have a solid understanding of how to engage in credible online research, you can encourage them to begin researching ways to enact their critical literacy understandings in meaningful ways.

The first step in researching for change is assisting students in narrowing and selecting their area of focus. Students might work in collaborative groups or pairs through asynchronous sharing of documents and brainstorms, or in a synchronous manner at preselected meeting times within the learning management system or conference call platforms. They might also elect to work independently based on their area of interest or needs within the online classroom setting. Regardless, you will want to provide students with platforms and strategies for identifying a topic of research, documenting their online research sources, maintaining notes, and brainstorming ideas for action.

A simple spreadsheet program or application can work wonders for organizing ideas and information throughout the research process. Assist students in crafting and maintaining such a spreadsheet to keep track of online search terms or phrases, important quotes, information or contact numbers, website addresses, and relevant citations. It is not uncommon for adolescent learners to struggle with organization skills. Therefore, it might be necessary to explicitly teach students how to design and maintain a spreadsheet through an online tutorial or synchronous modeling session.

Just as students in the traditional space might generate ideas for action projects that involve reaching out, contacting, or meeting with others involved in a variety of fields or professions, the same is true for virtual learners. However, unlike the traditional classroom setting, virtual teachers are limited in our ability to oversee and assist students in their efforts. In addition, students might find they want to speak with individuals who are separated by several hundred miles. For this reason, it is important to maintain open communication and provide prompt feedback when assisting students through their research and implementation. Encourage students to begin within their own community.

In what ways might they utilize what they have learned to promote positive change and action within their own community space? Encourage local engagement as you utilize communication methods highlighted in chapter 1, including maintaining connection with parents and families. Allow students autonomy in working through their ideas, but make them aware of any implications involved in taking action that might be significant to maintaining their safety, time, and money. Is their research likely to lead them to making calls or connections that could be financially costly to the family? Is there a way you might provide additional assistance in establishing contact with local organizations despite your distance from the student? Are there additional questions they might consider as they move forward in their brainstorming?

Create and Share

Once students have conducted their research and identified ideas for engaging within the community, it is time to assist them in creating and implementing their critical action with care and consideration. While there is a significant challenge in providing hands-on assistance through virtual channels, it is possible for virtual teachers to maintain connection and review of student efforts. One way to stay in the know is through student reflections and a portfolio of student work. A variety of online programs and platforms encourage consistent sharing and collaboration.

In addition to those shared in previous chapters, students can utilize platforms such as Seesaw, an online collaboration and portfolio tool, to promote student documentation and sharing with the virtual teacher and families alike. Students can import their reflections and work directly from platforms such as Google Drive, and utilize voice recording, drawing tools, video, and more to document and share their engagement work. Online portfolios or blogs give learners the space to maintain documentation of their critical engagement, and space to reflect on how this engagement speaks to their understanding of course texts, discussions, and activities. It also provides opportunity for classmates, teachers, and families to keep track of student efforts, critical engagement, and areas of need.

Chapter Eight

Assessing Reading Comprehension

In an ideal world, virtual learners would be motivated to log in to their online course each day, engage in meaningful ways with course content, communicate questions or concerns in an open and timely manner, and navigate the curriculum in such a way that they are empowered as learners. However, this is not always the case. Students approach the class with a myriad of individual needs, experiences, talents, interests, and more. At times, a rigid online curriculum or instructional approach inhibits students in their educational growth. There are times when students benefit from additional support, a unique approach to instruction, and adjustments to curriculum and practice. The key is effective monitoring and analysis of student performance and understanding. While teachers might assume students are progressing in an effective way through the course, it is important to take time to assess their learning so that you might continue to aid them in navigating the online platform and in their development as readers.

There are two approaches to assessment in the classroom: formative and summative. Formative reading assessment provides an ongoing glimpse into students' engagement, comprehension, and development as critical readers and consumers of text. Teachers utilize formative assessment on a continuing basis—to assess formation of knowledge. Taken at varying intervals throughout a course, formative assessments provide information and feedback that will help guide teachers in improving the quality of student learning, as well as the quality of the course (Dunn & Mulvenon, 2009). Summative reading assessments provide space to evaluate student mastery of course content and skills. In other words, formative assessments provide information about how a student is learning, while summative assessments document the learning that has taken place.

STRATEGIES FOR FORMATIVE READING ASSESSMENT

Exit Tickets

The traditional classroom schedule is often limiting—so much to teach and do, so little time in a given class period to do it. A popular method of quick formative assessment comes in the form of "exit tickets." Teachers may pose a question about the day's reading assignment or content, or simply ask students to share something they learned from the day's lesson. Students respond on a post-it note, scrap of paper, or whiteboard. This simple and efficient way of checking in on student understanding requires little time and effort, but holds the potential to offer a wealth of insight and information for the teacher.

There are ways of translating this check-in strategy to the virtual classroom. In a synchronous environment, the teacher can pose a question or prompt at the conclusion of the online learning session. Students can share their ideas via chat box, direct message, or by typing their response to the virtual whiteboard. Within an asynchronous environment, the teacher can include the prompt at the conclusion of a learning module or asynchronous lesson. Using SparkPost, teachers can also add visuals and graphics to exit tickets. Ask students to respond in either writing via email or text, or through video or audio using VoiceThread or Flipgrid. While responses will be staggered according to student engagement within the noted text or learning module, virtual exit tickets offer teachers a quick means of assessing student engagement, progress, and understanding of course material.

Student Reflections

Personal reflection can be a powerful thing. Taking time to consider one's own understanding, approach to learning, and areas of personal confusion can empower students as learners. In the traditional classroom, teachers can ask students to compose a reflective paper or engage in conferencing that highlights their key takeaways, engagement, goals, and perceptions of self as readers. Such reflection encourages meta-cognition for students, but it also provides insight for the teacher. Through student reflection of learning, teachers are able to witness the aspects of the curriculum or the text that stand out to learners, the instructional approaches that you feel work best for their needs as learners, and perhaps the elements of the curriculum that require additional time or attention.

If working within a synchronous platform, or through open communicative approaches to instruction, virtual teachers can conference with students in a one-on-one format to ask questions that generate student reflection. Simply schedule a time to chat, select a platform in which to "meet," and document student response. Then, examine each aspect of the student's reflection to evaluate understanding of course material, as well as self-perceptions as a learner. What did that student choose to highlight? What appears to be missing? What might this mean for the student's formative knowledge, as well as your own approach to reading instruction?

Teachers working within an asynchronous classroom can also take advantage of student reflection as a means of formative reading assessment. Simply direct students to complete a written reflection and submit their work for review and response. Provide guiding questions such as, "What takeaways do you have from the reading this week?" "What questions come to mind based on what you read and took away from class this week?" and "What instruction or information from this week's module assisted you in learning?" You might conclude your guided reflection with an opportunity for students to share anything else they want you to know about their reading, engagement, or understanding for the week. Following review, encourage students to continue reflecting and sharing within your provided feedback and questions.

STRATEGIES FOR SUMMATIVE READING ASSESSMENT

Traditional Summative

Summative assessments are implemented at the end of a chapter or unit of study as a means of gauging individual student learning and understanding of specific concepts and topics. More times than not, these summative assessments are composed in traditional formats: true-false questions, multiple-choice questions, matching, fill-in-the blanks, and essay or short responses. In the traditional classroom, a teacher passes out the assessment, a student completes it using a pen or pencil, the teacher collects and grades. This common summative assessment practice can be easily transferred to the online context using free assessment platforms such as Kahoot!, Edulastic, ProProfs, Quia, and Quizlet, to name a few.

Through the use of a platform to create summative assessments for students, virtual teachers have an opportunity to engage learners in a way that traditional paper assessments cannot. As virtual teachers create traditional summative assessments via technology platforms like the ones mentioned above, they can also include images, links to visuals, and videos or sound, which traditional classroom summative assessments cannot do. By including these components in a summative assessment, virtual teachers can move students past the simple recall of information, and toward analyzing, evaluating, and synthesizing.

While a pen or pencil is the common tool used for completing traditional summative assessments, in the online classroom, the virtual teacher has many options. Virtual students could be asked to type in answers to short responses, or craft an essay. They might also be asked to provide oral answers, recording them using the microphone on their computer. Virtual teachers could also ask students to indicate answers using signs and symbols, as opposed to words. For example, they could ask students to insert an arrow to connect words and their definitions, or arrows and curved lines to show connections between concepts and ideas.

Verbal Assessment

When determining what a student has learned, writing is no doubt the most commonly practiced form of assessment. Students write to demonstrate learning through essays, lab reports, or short responses to content questions posed by the teacher. But there is another format that teachers can implement as a summative assessment—verbal. In the traditional classroom, verbal summative assessments are usually conducted face to face, between the teacher and the student. During this conference, the teacher poses questions or prompts and the student responds orally.

As the student is providing answers, the teacher is listening, taking notes, and either asking follow-up questions for clarity, or affirming the correctness of the answer. In blended classrooms, teachers can use technology to capture students' reading comprehension, requiring students to respond verbally through a platform or recording device on a classroom computer. Students could record their responses and upload them to an assignment link on the class web page, or send it directly to the teacher via email. In the virtual classroom, verbal assessments could be easily implemented in a similar fashion to the blended learning environment.

Verbal summative assessments require students to demonstrate learning through verbal communication. This communication can occur in both asynchronous and synchronous contexts in the online classroom. In an asynchronous format, teachers can approach verbal summative assessments in several ways. Using an application like Flipgrid, virtual teachers could post a video asking students to respond to a question or series of questions. Students could respond to the teacher directly through Flipgrid.

As the teacher watches and listens to the student's responses, Flipgrid allows the teacher to respond and provide feedback in the form of follow-up questions for clarity, or affirmation of correctness. Another approach could be simply posting a question or series of questions on the course page and asking students to record their responses via the microphone on their computer or through a platform such as VoiceThread. Students could then email the file directly to the teacher or post it in an assignment link.

In a synchronous setting, the virtual teacher could arrange a date and time to assess a student. The teacher and student could log on to a video conferencing platform and, through real-time interaction, the teacher could pose questions or prompts and students could respond. This format most replicates the face-to-face verbal summative assessments practiced in the traditional classroom. If a video conference is not an option, a phone call can serve as another means of synchronous summative assessment.

No matter which approach a virtual teacher uses to verbally assess what a student has learned, there are several reasons why verbal summative assessments are beneficial in the virtual classroom. Because online students are separated by time and space, virtual teachers do not have the capability to watch students take assessments. As such, verbal summative assessments help to ensure academic integrity. Additionally, through verbal assessments, virtual teachers can listen to students read prompts and/or questions, as well as their responses, as a way to gauge fluency.

Show Me What You Read

In all the assessments discussed so far in this chapter, each have been created and administered by the teacher. But there is another approach to summative assessments that place the student in charge—visual projects. Research has supported the use of visual arts as a means of assessing reading comprehension (Grant et al., 2008; Livingston, 2005; Miller & Hopper, 2010). Using visual arts as a form of summative assessment of reading comprehension "can offer an alternative that accommodates a variety of working styles and engages students in critical thinking skills" (Holdren, 2012, p. 692).

While a visual project can help a virtual teacher gauge comprehension on the surface, we suggest making this approach a higher-order one by requiring students to write or verbally describe the visual in terms of how it relates to the topic or concept being assessed, thus demonstrating critical thinking. For example, a student reading *The Hate U Give* (2017) by Angie Thomas in an English class to explore the theme of home could create a guided tour of the homes of the characters and the places where important events in the book took place (see figure 8.1). Or, a student reading the same book in a social studies class to explore activism and justice could create a hand-drawn visual representation of the theme(s) on a poster board, noting specific characters and their actions, and including direct quotes from the text (see figure 8.2).

Below is a list of other forms of visual projects that virtual teachers can assign, or allow students to choose from:

- *Book Trailer*. Make a book trailer for the book you read using Movie Maker, iMovie, Animoto, Prezi, or any other software program.
- *Characters' Poetry Choices*. Identify three specific characters and find a poem for each of them that you believe they would like. Write an explanation for why you think these poems suit the characters; read them to the

Figure 8.1. Sample student-guided tour of the homes in *The Hate U Give*. Created by the authors using Storyboard That

class. Variation: Pick out poetry that reflects something about the book's theme or setting.
- *Collage*. On a poster board, or using a blank Word document, make a collage that represents major characters and events in the book you read. Use pictures and words clipped from magazines in your collage. Include a detailed written explanation of what the pictures and/or words mean.
- *Diorama*. Make a shoebox diorama of a scene from the book you read. Write a detailed explanation of the scene and attach it to the diorama.
- *Interview*. Pretend you are a magazine or newspaper reporter, and record an interview with one of the characters in the book you read. Use a written script to guide you, and then write the article resulting from the interview. Note: If a classmate has read the same book, you might make this a two-person project with one person as the reporter and the other as the character in the book.
- *Models*. Make models of three objects (either physically or three-dimensionally using a technology application) that were important in the book you read. Tell why each object was important in the book.
- *Monologue*. Pretend that you are one of the characters in the book you read. You can record a monologue (one person talking) of that character telling his or her experiences, or perform it live. It is helpful to write out a script ahead of time. Practice using emotion, voice, and other voice inflections.

Figure 8.2. Sample student visual presentation on the themes of justice and activism in *The Hate U Give*. Courtesy of the authors

- *Painting.* Pretend you are Bob Ross and paint a picture in front of the class that explains the contents or setting of your book, without spoiling the ending.
- *Songwriting.* Write a song with lyrics that represent the book, its characters, or the setting. Perform the song either live or on tape, giving the class the lyrics so everyone can follow along.
- *Television Report.* You are a television news reporter. Videotape and present an on-the-scene news report based on an incident from the book.
- *Yearbook Snapshots.* Illustrate your in-depth understanding of four characters in your novel by imagining what they were like in high school. Capture the essence of them, their values, beliefs, and other characteristics by carefully selecting all the information that would go under their picture in a yearbook. Mount all four pictures, and write the appropriate information under each picture. Include the following information: 1) nickname; 2) activities, clubs, sports they played and what year (1, 2, 3, 4) in school; 3) a class mock award such as the "class clown"; 4) a quotation that shows something about the person and what is important to him or her; 5) favorites (colors, food, etc.); 6) a book that has had the greatest impact on them; 7) voted "most-likely-to?"; and 8) plans after high school.

In the virtual classroom, the use of visual projects can be approached in several ways. In chapter 2, we discussed student choice in the classroom. This form of assessment offers virtual students an opportunity to make academic decisions, as they would be allowed to choose which project they wanted to complete. Or the virtual teacher could assign a specific visual project for all students to complete. Whichever approach the virtual teacher implements, we suggest that they include a second complement to all visual assessments—explanation. Ask students to provide either a written or verbal explanation of their visual project as a way to further demonstrate reading comprehension and critical thinking skills.

In addition to determining who will decide on the visual summative assessment project, the virtual teacher must also decide how the student project will be shared. In an asynchronous setting, students can create a visual summative assessment project and upload it to an assignment link on the course webpage, or they can email it directly to the teacher. The teacher could view the visual project and assess it using a rubric. In chapter 1 we discussed book talks as a way to build community and get students interested in reading.

As an alternative, students could present their projects in teams. Students could be assigned to a team and required to post their visual assessment and explanation in the team discussion group. Teammates could be asked to view their teammates' projects and written/verbal explanations and then, using the assessment rubric, assess their teammates and provide feedback. In a synchronous setting, the student can present the visual summative assessment and verbal explanation directly to the teacher through a virtual conference session.

In this format, the teacher could provide immediate feedback to the student. Or, students could be assigned to a team that meets at a specific time and share their visual assessments and explanations. Teammates could also provide immediate feedback through this format. Additionally, in a synchronous format, teammates could be required to discuss the text in more depth, answering a series of prompts provided by the teacher. If each member of the team is reading different texts, students could discuss differences or commonalities within the various texts.

Chapter Nine

Engaging in the Writing Process

Writing is a complex and demanding skill that is foundational to a person's success both in and out of school. Writing also requires vulnerability. It is an act of bravery to put our words to paper, and then share those words with others. Writing opens us up to interpretation and potential judgment. It is no wonder that even the most prolific of authors face a state of intimidation when it comes time to compose and publish. But effective writing just doesn't happen by putting pen to paper or cursor to document. It is a process that students must progress through and practice.

Literacy use for adolescents has become increasingly more complex and demanding (Alvermann, 2002) and as such, literacy instruction is essential for students because it helps them shape and use literacy in ways that lead to meaningful learning. Specific to writing, Kelly Gallagher (2006) notes that, "in this increasingly demanding world of literacy, it has become critical that students know how to write effectively. From the requirements of standardized tests to those of the wired workplace, the ability to write well has become a necessity" (p. 4). Because much of the communication that transpires in the online classroom occurs through writing, "teaching online privileges writing in ways that traditional classes cannot" (Harrington et al., 2000, p. 8).

Writing in online spaces opens up opportunities for students to practice multiple forms of writing, for multiple purposes. But before teachers can lead students through these forms and purposes, you must remember the process through which students must navigate as they produce written works. In this chapter, we offer strategies for guiding virtual students through the writing process.

BRAINSTORMING

The initial step in the writing process is a crucial step. Before putting pen to paper, or cursor to document, writers need to take time and generate ideas. Many call this process brainstorming. Others kindly refer to it as brain dumping. The key is simply providing space to get the creative juices flowing. Whether this means identifying a topic or theme of focus, considering directions for one's selected focus, or perhaps considering key ideas for inclusion into one's writing, you want to provide the time and space to generate such ideas, reflect on what you've considered, and narrow your focus before you begin outlining and drafting your work. For some students, the brainstorming process is essential to beginning their work in an effective manner. When they tell themselves, "I have nothing to write," or "I can't do this," it may be that a brainstorm is just the ticket in helping them transform "I can't" to "I've got this!"

The online world hosts a plethora of applications and programs that students can use as they engage in the brainstorming process. Students who prefer to work independently can utilize a word processing program or online processing program, such as Google Docs, to freewrite on a provided topic, phrase, or idea. They might set a timer for five minutes and simply type any words or phrases that come to mind. Once time has elapsed, they can begin reading through their work, highlighting key terms that stand out as potential ideas for writing.

If a single round of freewriting isn't enough, students can narrow down their brainstorming ideas generated in the first version, then take another five minutes to build on the key terms they identified the first time through. Once they have potential ideas, students can group and organize their ideas using a spreadsheet. Such programs provide the same space for generating and sifting through initial thoughts as traditional pen and paper, but with the added benefit of digital recording.

If students want to engage in collaborative brainstorming—either synchronously or asynchronously—they can share their work on the aforementioned programs, or work together using online mind mapping applications such as MindMeister or FreeMind. Such applications allow students to work independently and share their maps with one another, or co-create in real time to comment on one another's ideas, finalize decisions regarding brainstorming ideas and selections, and make changes to ideas before moving forward in the writing process. They also provide a platform for crafting a brainstorm through multiple modalities or formats, thus providing options for students as they navigate the brainstorming process.

As teachers, you also understand that students may encounter a block when generating initial ideas for their work. In a traditional classroom, you can approach students you identify to be struggling, offer questions or advice, and help them get started. The asynchronous nature of the virtual classroom has the potential to limit our in-the-moment availability to identify and assist students in getting started with their writing process. For this reason, students may benefit from online programs to help them generate an initial thought or idea related to the writing topic at hand. Programs such as HubSpot, Idea Generator, and Portent's Content Idea Generator provide space for writers to share single words or phrases to generate potential ideas and titles that can aid in the brainstorming and planning process. A simple online search of "idea generators" will yield a range of results to help writers get started with a topic or focus of interest or relevance to the writing task.

OUTLINING

Traditional Linear Outlines

Once students have brainstormed, they now need to organize their thoughts in a way that will lead them to craft a logical and coherent piece of writing. One strategy that can assist them in this process is outlining. In the virtual classroom, there are several approaches to outlining that can be implemented to guide students through this component of the writing process. One such approach is using an online graphic organizer that replicates those commonly utilized in the traditional classroom (figure 9.1).

In an asynchronous format, virtual teachers could provide an outline template as a Word document, requiring students to simply fill in the blanks. Once completed, students could then send this outline to the teacher for review. In a synchronous format, students could work in teams to complete an outline via Google Docs.

Another approach to guiding virtual students through the outlining process is to utilize interactive online outlining platforms. In chapter 2 we discussed the need for student choice in the classroom. Through platforms such as Little Outliner, Evernote, or Microsoft OneNote, all of which are free, students have an opportunity to choose the format of their outline. These platforms also allow students to create outlines collaboratively and to offer feedback on each other's outlines.

Once students have organized their thoughts into outline format, teachers can move students forward in their thinking and planning of their written piece by having them focus on each specific section of the outline in more depth. An online interactive outlining tool that virtual students can utilize to accomplish this is WorkFlowy. This free tool contains a zoom feature that allows students to zoom into each section in isolation, helping to reduce the distractions of the other sections. As students zoom in, they have the opportunity to add additional information to the outline. The information added will appear as a comment, so the outline doesn't become congested or diffi-

Outline Template

Paper Topic: ______________________________

I. INTRODUCTION

Possible ideas for introduction (hook)

____
____
____

II. BODY

A. Main Point:

Examples/Details

a. ______________________________
b. ______________________________
c. ______________________________

B. Main Point:

Examples/Details

a. ______________________________
b. ______________________________
c. ______________________________

C. Main Point:

Examples/Details

a. ______________________________
b. ______________________________
c. ______________________________

III. CONCLUSION

Restate Thesis/ Main Idea in new terms

____
____
____

Offer a resolution, suggestion, or recommendation

____
____
____

Figure 9.1. Sample outline template. ***Created by the authors***

cult to follow. Additionally, this tool allows students to add hashtags (#) within each section of the outline that can serve as reminders for what is still needed. For example, a student may add #addmore where they feel they need to provide more supporting evidence. The best part is that the hashtags they add are all searchable, allowing them to quickly locate areas of their outline that need attention without having to physically search through each section individually.

Visual Outlines

While some students work well with traditional linear outlines as described above, other students may find visual outlines more helpful in organizing their brainstorming information. In chapter 7 we shared how students can use mind maps as a strategy for visual note-taking. But mind maps can also be used as an outlining strategy in both asynchronous and synchronous approaches.

Using mind maps as an outline tool, students can physically see relationships and connections between ideas and concepts easier than through a traditional outline, as mind mapping allows for the use of connectors such as arrows and lines. Students using an interactive platform like MindMeister (discussed in chapter 7) can move these connectors without having to erase or move information around. Additionally, through a mind mapping outline, students can add pictures or visuals as supporting evidence, which can lead to the discovery of more information. Students can also add symbols and even colors to their outline as a way to indicate sections of their outline that are completed or may need more support.

DRAFTING

Word Processing Programs

Students have now brainstormed and outlined their essay or story, and are now ready to begin the writing process itself. While it is likely common knowledge that traditional word processing programs can aid students in drafting and refining their writing, we would be remiss if we didn't acknowledge this tool for virtual classrooms. Students can take advantage of the word processing programs that often accompany the purchase or use of their devices in drafting their work. Such programs provide the basics necessary for crafting, revising, commenting on, and sharing student drafts.

Students searching for a free alternative to the traditional word processing programs can take advantage of online processing platforms such as LibreOffice or Google Docs. These free alternatives provide access to tools similar to those of purchased programs, with the benefit of limited or no cost to the virtual learner.

Some students benefit from limited options or interference. The virtual classroom has the potential to overwhelm learners as they initiate their drafting process. So many options, links, and distractions can hamper the ability to focus in on the task at hand. For this reason, it might also benefit writers to identify online platforms or resources that limit distractions. For example, FocusWriter is a free online program that lets students access a hideaway interface as they engage in the drafting process. Such programs help students fully immerse in the drafting process by limiting on-screen interruptions.

Writing-to-Text Programs

Learning within the virtual classroom setting does not have to mean surrendering a student's preference for handwritten work. Those who prefer to stick with handwriting their drafts can utilize an online program to either write directly onto their device, or transfer their handwritten work from paper to type. There are a variety of free programs that transform images of handwritten text to font. While some programs are easier to navigate, or more accurate in transforming writing to text, teachers and students can research up-to-date programs to find the one that translates well to the current learning platform, course content, and student needs. There are also programs such as OneNote that offer a way to directly handwrite a draft and have it immediately translated to type.

Speech-to-Text Programs

Some students may prefer to generate ideas and begin drafting work through a speech-to-text application. Such programs promote personal reflection and can help capture a student's ideas with greater ease and simplicity. Online speech-to-text programs, such as Google Docs voice typing, Speechnotes, and Apple Dictation are free applications compatible with a variety of devices. Writers can simply speak out their ideas, capture their draft in the moment, and take time to review the transcription as they prepare to engage in the revision and editing process. Such programs can also benefit learners who are preparing to work in a language other than their first or primary language.

REVISION

Instructor Feedback

One-on-one support from the classroom instructor can be incredibly helpful for students as they prepare to engage in the revision process. While you may not be able to sit down face to face with your virtual learners, you can certainly take advantage of all that the virtual platform has to offer in terms of reviewing, discussing, and providing feedback on student work. Virtual teachers can utilize the synchronous contact methods suggested throughout previous chapters to reach out and connect with students in real time to read, discuss, and assist writers as they transition from their initial draft toward a finished product. Teachers can employ a variety of free online scheduling applications, such as Doodle or PickTime, to schedule one-on-one writing conferences with learners. Scheduling a writing conference promotes student response to communication efforts, and helps to ensure time committed to engaging in quality conversation with each virtual learner.

If synchronous conferencing is not feasible, virtual teachers can utilize the asynchronous platforms shared in previous chapters to provide written, voice, or video comments and suggestions to assist students throughout the reflection and revision process. While asynchronous writing conferencing is not exactly the same as synchronous conversation, today's virtual applications provide avenues for back-and-forth connection that can help students navigate the review and revision process.

Collaborative Feedback Groups

In the traditional classroom, teachers may encourage student revision through collaboration with the teacher and peers. The same can apply to the virtual learning space. Whether working in a synchronous or asynchronous setting, students can share their drafts with peers on the same platforms described in chapter 6.

If working synchronously, students can share their feedback and questions using the microphone or chat box within the LMS or conference discussion application. Students can move into breakout rooms, or meet as a small group on a virtual meeting site; display their work on a shared screen, or share their work via email or within the online program; and take time to provide one-on-one questions and insights. As with any classroom, the key is assisting students in understanding and navigating the peer feedback process. It is beneficial to take time to explicitly teach students how to serve as a reviewer, ask questions, and provide feedback that is positive and helpful in nature.

If working asynchronously, students can post their work, giving others opportunities to edit or comment on the work. Whether this means sharing work through email or the learning management system and responding via discussion thread, embedded comments, or voice/video discussions, the key is providing students access to one another's work, setting clear expectations and timelines for responding to one another's ideas, and encouraging helpful discussion in the process.

Revision Process

After students have an opportunity to review their work, discuss their drafts with their teacher and peers, and reflect on their work, it is time to begin revising their drafts. Virtual platforms such as Google Docs provide students space to revise initial drafts while maintaining access to earlier drafts along the way. Word processing programs provide options for tracking changes, thereby promoting the revision process without negating any previous work. And, students can be encouraged to save work according to draft numbers as another way of maintaining a trail for work in progress.

Teachers can share out revision checklists with students as a means of scaffolding the revision process. Students can access the checklist as they work, documenting the questions they have considered and the process they have followed in revising their initial work. Students can also utilize the voice recording options noted in the drafting process as a way to document their own ideas and considerations for change as they progress through revising their independent work.

EDITING

Collaborative Editing Groups

Just as students can work in asynchronous and synchronous ways to share drafts and suggestions for revision, they can do the same for peer editing of their work. Online platforms allow students to exchange, view, comment on, and suggest updates to one another's writing samples. One strategy for utilizing such platforms for peer editing is to translate a collaborative color-coded editing technique to the virtual classroom. In the traditional classroom, students can sit together in collaborative groups, exchange papers, and utilize particular colored pencils or markers to identify designated editing needs within a set of papers. Teachers can utilize this same strategy in the virtual setting through Google Classroom, email transmission of word processing documents, or similar applications.

Assign each student an editing role. For instance, one student can be tasked with checking for standard sentence structure. Another student might be assigned the role of identifying problematic verb tense. And, another student might be assigned the job of editing punctuation. In addition to a role, each student will be assigned a particular color of font. Utilizing track changes or a similar feature, students can then review their peers' work, using the font color associated with their editing role, and work to identify the editing needs of their group members. Not only do students receive valuable feedback from their classmates regarding their own work, they gain insight into particular editing techniques based on their assigned role.

PUBLISHING

One of the beautiful realities of teaching in a virtual context is immediate access to a worldwide audience! There's no reason students can't publish and share their hard work with an audience that extends beyond the classroom space. Take advantage of this incredible opportunity, and give your students an authentic audience that will provide purpose, enjoyment, and celebration for their completed work.

You can enhance student voice and choice throughout the publication process by helping students research their publication options. Help them to identify platforms appropriate for the purpose, form, and intended audience for their work. Ensure they consider the benefits, costs, and potential challenges to publishing their work online. Some important questions for students to consider include:

- What is the format and purpose of my writing?
- Who is my intended audience?
- What are my options for publication? (books, journals, newspapers, websites, blogs, etc.)
- Of the options I have selected, which are free and accessible to me?
- Who will have access to my published work?
- Who will have access to comment on my published work?
- What are the potential outcomes of publishing my work to my selected location?

Whether you choose to share student work on a class blog, website, or more public options, be sure to obtain student and family consent. Students should be fully aware of where their work will be displayed, and how it might be shared or utilized as a result of publication. In addition, do your research. Take note of access to the selected publication—who is likely to view student work, who is able to comment on or share student work, and what can you do to best protect your students and their ideas in this public space. You might also take time to explicitly teach students important skills in publishing their work to the virtual platform, as well as critical thinking skills in determining the best platform and means of sharing their work online. Help students to see the value, as well as considerations, in sharing their work on a public platform. This is an ideal time to help learners understand more about their rights as authors, ways to maintain reasonable anonymity, and internet safety.

Once you have worked with students to identify an outlet for publication, you might take time to ensure that their final work meets publication guidelines. If possible, encourage students to select a space for publication at the start of their drafting process. This way, they are more likely to have met specific guidelines prior to the publication stage. Otherwise, encourage students to revisit their work, restructuring or editing as necessary to make sure they meet the requirements specified by the online publication host.

Chapter Ten

Engaging Online Students in Multiple Forms of Writing

Authors approach their work with purpose and intent. The key is understanding the objective of one's work and identifying the structure, modality, audience, and outlet for each unique text. It is important that students also understand the purpose and form of their own writing so that it might take shape and meet the intended goal of the mode in which they are being asked to write.

Technology has brought about new communication paradigms that have changed the way we define writing (Gunter & Kenny, 2008). As a result, there is a need "for students to design, produce and present multimodal texts as representations of learning" (Edwards-Groves, 2011, p. 49). For virtual classrooms, where students are utilizing computers and technologies as a medium through which to produce written text, there is a need to examine the ways in which virtual teachers can take what they know about writing modes and forms and translate this knowledge to the digital context.

There are multiple modes and forms of writing that students experience in the classroom; "modes" refers to the type of writing, while "form" refers to the specific structure used to produce the mode (see figure 10.1). Some modes and forms of writing are practiced within specific content areas more often than others (i.e., reports in science, literary analysis in English language arts, cause and effect in history). However, students will write in all these modes and forms at several points throughout their schooling experience and beyond.

The strategies we present in this chapter can engage students in the online modalities of writing. While we do not address each mode separately, we do present strategies that can be utilized across multiple modes of writing. While most, if not all, teachers now require students to draft formal essays

Mode	Purpose	Forms
Personal	Explore thoughts and feelings	• Blog • Journal • Discussion Board Posts
Narrative	Tell a story	• Autobiography • Biography
Expository	Inform or explain	• Cause and Effect Essay • Compare and Contrast Essay • How-to Essay • Explanatory Essay
Argumentative	Convince or evaluate	• Argument Essay • Problem – Solution Essay
Response to Literature	Review or analyze a work of literature: poem, movie, play, short story, book	• Literary Analysis • Book Report • Movie or Book Review • Discussion Board Posts
Research	Explore a topic using multiple sources and sharing findings	• Research Paper • Summary • Report
Creative	Artistic Use of Language	• Story • Poem • Song • Play • Artwork
Professional	Communicate in the workplace	• Email • Report • Memo • Resume • Proposal • Letter

Figure 10.1. Mode, purpose, and forms of writing. *Adapted from Thoughtful Learning*

and research reports through Word documents, the strategies we shared in chapter 9 address these modes of writing. As such, the strategies presented in this chapter address modes beyond research and essay.

STRATEGIES FOR ENGAGING STUDENTS IN MULTIPLE FORMS OF ONLINE WRITING

Journaling

Sometimes students need opportunities to reflect about what they read in a personal, informal way. Journaling can be a great form of writing to help students record their thoughts, feelings, connections, and even confusion about a text or topic. Given the personal nature of journaling, when students write in this form, they don't need to worry about who is going to read it, or what criticisms may stem from someone else's interpretations of their understanding—or misunderstanding. And because journal writing is a personal form of writing, it can be utilized across all content areas.

There are also unintentional benefits to personal journal writing in the classroom beyond getting students in the habit of reflecting through writing. In addition to encouraging reflection and documenting a student's feelings, connections, or questions about a text, journal writing itself can improve writing skills. Every time students write, they individualize instruction, as the act of reflective writing may generate ideas, observations, or further emotions (Fulwiler, 1980). While personal journal writing can bring about the aforementioned benefits, students can also use their personal journal writings as a tool for academic writing. In chapter 9 we discussed the process of brainstorming in writing. Journaling as a personal writing strategy can be used as a brainstorming tool as well.

In traditional classrooms, students often undertake personal journaling by physically writing in a notebook with a pen or pencil. These notebooks can be kept in the classroom, and the teacher can refer to them as a means of gauging students' connections, perspectives, misconceptions, or questions about texts or topics. Additionally, students can physically revisit the journals as a way to track understanding and content knowledge development. In the virtual classroom, journal notebooks can be utilized in much the same way. Instead of journaling in traditional notebooks, virtual students can journal through interactive digital notebooks.

As virtual teachers look to implement journal writing in their content area, they need to keep several characteristics of the interactive journal in mind. First, the journal itself should be one that is easy to navigate. For example, you might want your students to use a journal application that is either in calendar format or one that allows them to create unique, individualized headings. Second, you want to make sure that the journal is accessible to you, especially if you are going to use the journal as a formative assessment. There are several free applications that online students who are journaling can use that meet both these criteria. For example, glimpses and Evernote offer students an online interactive journal that allows learners to not only create written posts, but to include photos, drawings, pictures, or even audio to support written text. Evernote even has a feature that allows students to search their journal for keywords. Virtual teachers can gain access to student journals in these applications through a shareable link.

In chapters 7 and 9 we discussed creating visual text as a note-taking and brainstorming strategy. For students who are more artistic in nature, recording reflections, connections, questions, and other thoughts through visual text in their journal may be an option. Using an application like Journalist, students can actually draw and/or physically write on the screen using the app's drawing tools, and both will transfer to their journal. Teachers can access the journal through a shareable link.

Blogs

In the traditional classroom, teachers often find themselves asking students to engage in informal conversation or writing. Through modalities such as journaling, as described above, teachers are able to capture student understanding in words or illustrations. You can do the same in the online classroom through the use of blogs. A blog is a website designed to share informal, or diary-style, ideas and information. We might think of it as the virtual version of a student journal or writer's notebook. If you search for blogs, you are likely to find them pertaining to any and every idea under the sun! As virtual teachers, you can utilize blogs to encourage your students as writers in a number of ways.

To begin, consider the role and purpose of blogs within your own classroom. If utilizing blogs for the purpose of brainstorming or informal journaling, you might consider maintaining a private blog setting for your students. Blogs have the ability to serve as public or private means of maintaining and sharing out one's work. If student work is not intended for publication, or is not ready to be shared in a public domain, ensure your class blog is set to private viewing. If you choose to host a blog that reflects student work in a public space, maintain awareness of what your students are posting as it relates to private or contact information. It is also important to consider who can access the blog or comment on student work.

Another important consideration is the online location you select to host your class blog. There are a variety of free domains intended for educational blogging purposes. For instance, Edublogs and Weebly are two current programs that provide space for students and teachers to learn more about the blogging process, create websites that meet their educational needs, and post work in a private or public setting. A simple online search can assist you in identifying the blogging site suited to your individual classroom needs.

Students can utilize blogs for a variety of purposes within their writing. You can have students engage in private blogging to journal about their day, the contents of a text or lesson, reflect on their current learning, or to respond to prompts or areas of writing focus. For example, in the traditional classroom, teachers might engage students in an assortment of prompt writing to engage their narrative, expository, or creative writing skills. Teachers within the virtual space can do the same through online blogging. You can post a topic or prompt, and ask students to respond to the class page, or to their own page housed on the classroom blog platform. You might also engage in blogging as a way to publish student writing. As noted in chapter 9, the virtual classroom provides a world of opportunity to broadcast student ideas and provide a wider audience for student work.

Discussion Board Posts

The traditional classroom provides time and space for students to engage in collaborative writing and discussion. Turn and talks, partner shares, and small-group learning work wonders for engaging students in writing and discussion aimed at collaborative understanding and growth. In the virtual space, educators will often try to utilize discussion boards as a parallel form of collaborative learning and writing engagement. Discussion boards serve to engage learners in asynchronous discussion surrounding a variety of topics and for a wide array of purposes within their virtual classroom space. Discussion board posts allow students to engage in informal writing that promotes critical consideration and collaboration between the teacher and learner, as well as among classmates. The teacher can begin the online discussion by posting a question related to the course material or module of learning. Or, have students take the lead in sharing a question or topic of interest, and then generating the noted question into an initial discussion board post.

From there, have students reply to one another by sharing their thoughts, questions, and interpretations as replies. The key is finding ways to effectively engage students in this form of writing in a way that is meaningful and purposeful. It is very easy for learners to simply log in, post a response to the first thread they encounter on the discussion board, and then disengage from the asynchronous discussion. Some ways of encouraging written response, reflection, and continued discussion is setting parameters for student engagement. Inform students about your objective for the discussion thread, why they are participating in the thread, and the purpose of continued participation in their understanding of course material. Try to identify discussion points that will prompt student writing and participation. And, ensure that students are aware of their role in actively participating within the discussion board. How are they being assessed? How frequently are they expected to participate? What are the expectations, and suggested tips for ensuring participation and engagement?

Encourage students to read through the threads and replies generated by their classmates. Seek out ways to encourage them to reply and do so in respectful ways. It is important that students feel safe in sharing their ideas through written responses and replies. You want them to understand that it is okay to disagree or question the ideas shared by others, but there are ways of doing so that maintain respect and safety, rather than engaging in an aggressive or hostile manner. In addition, be certain to keep an eye on the discussion board. You want to know what students are sharing, how they are participating, if the objective of your discussion post is indeed being met through this method of engagement, and if there are ways you might enhance or adjust the posting to better meet the needs of your online learners. As in the traditional classroom, if your intended purpose is not being met, or you see that the writing reflected within the discussion board is not meeting your course objectives, it is okay to make necessary adjustments to the practice in an effort to address the needs of the learner.

Creative Writing Spaces

Creative writing can be incredibly fun and engaging. It can also be a source of intimidation or fear for our students. When students have a solid understanding of narrative structure, character development, and confidence in their abilities to produce a piece of creative writing, they are more likely to actively seek out and engage in creative writing inside and outside of the classroom. If you want to tap into the skills, mind, and heart of *all* of your online learners, you need to ensure that your virtual classroom is a space that nourishes student autonomy, self-efficacy, and development as creative writers. There are a variety of spaces online for generating, hosting, and publishing youth creative writing.

National Novel Writing Month (NaNoWriMo) is a national, internet-based effort that takes place each November to encourage participants to write, or complete, a creative writing piece of their own. NaNoWriMo Young Writers Program is a free, online writing program that provides educators a space to encourage students as creative writers through online learning modules, student workbooks, and a classroom dashboard where teachers can hold discussions, monitor student writing, and engage learners in writing challenges apart from the NaNoWriMo program. Teachers can create as many digital classrooms as necessary, and enroll students in the program through a unique classroom access code. Students can set their own writing goals—unique to the needs and desires of the student—and begin writing. Students earn digital badges as they progress toward their creative writing goal. They can also update their goals based on their progress throughout the month.

Programs such as NaNoWriMo encourage learners to begin and engage in creative writing in a consistent manner through personal challenge, fun, and imagination. Rather than worry about revision or editing—though that is always an option based on the objectives of the class—students can unleash their imagination and develop their confidence as writers. In the end, teachers and students can print out their completed work, or use the month as a starting point for something greater.

Collaborative Creative Writing Spaces

In the traditional space, students often build on creative stories or work with a line-by-line or section-by-section focus. For instance, students might begin a creative text, pass their work along to a classmate, and then build on the ideas of their partner to co-author a single text. The same works in the virtual classroom. A simple and effective way of translating collaborative writing from the traditional space to the virtual context is through online collaborative writing platforms. For example, Google Classroom is a fantastic tool for engaging multiple writers in either synchronous or asynchronous collaborative creative writing work. Share out a document with your students, assign each writer a font color, and provide a starting prompt, topic, or image. Separate the document into sections according to the number of students participating in the collaborative activity. Have each student type out the initial statement or section of their creative piece. Then, have students rotate to the next student's assigned section to continue the story. As the teacher, you can monitor student progress and participation based on each version of the document, as well as student changes or updates to the creative work.

Publishing Spaces

Finally, there are spaces where students can take finalized creative work and publish it to obtain feedback from others. The key is to identify a site that hosts material appropriate to your classroom content and audience needs, and does so in a way that further encourages students as writers, rather than cultivate a climate of competition and disenfranchisement. For instance, sites such as Youth Voices, Teen Ink, and Write the World enable students to share their creative work and gain feedback from peers from around the world. Youth Voices contains direct links to particular schools involved in the online program, and accessibility to podcasts, nonfiction works, literature, poems, and more. In addition, the site offers students information and templates for responding to peer work as a means of encouraging thoughtful response and reading analysis.

Teen Ink contains access to a variety of creative writing genres, art and photography, as well as summer programs and contests. Write the World provides a platform for educators to create a private writing group within their online classroom. Teachers can mentor students throughout the writing process, assess student writing and development, and encourage students to develop their unique digital writing portfolios. Once students are ready to share their work with a global audience, teachers can assist students in publishing their work through Write the World, compete in a variety of writing competitions, and benefit from peer review from students outside the confines of the single virtual classroom space.

Writing Reviews

Book Reviews

In addition to informal and creative modes of online writing, teachers can encourage students as critical readers and writers through the writing and sharing of online book reviews. Students within the traditional classroom often engage in literary analysis and review. Following the reading of a text, students might write a formal essay, analysis paper, or book talk to share out with the class through a class-wide presentation or open discussion. As you translate this concept to the virtual platform, students have the opportunity to share their reading analysis and reflection on a work with a worldwide audience.

You might begin with a virtual class book review group. Websites and applications, such as Goodreads, provide opportunities for readers to share and track what they are reading, provide recommendations for others, and reflect on their reading by sharing a personalized review of the text. Students can formulate a plan for their reading, engage in written analysis, and publish their review through the group's "shared shelf," and even provide video uploads as they collaborate and discuss the books together. The merging of reading and writing in this particular way encourages students as prolific readers while also promoting their writing skills in both formal and informal ways. The teacher can serve as the group moderator, or assign this role to students on a rotating basis depending on the objectives of the reading or writing assignment within the online course.

Applications of this nature promote book review analysis, as well as collaboration, questioning, and thoughtful reflection about one's reading tendencies, preferences, and focus. A student can serve as moderator to pose a question regarding the text, suggest a particular passage for reflection, or call on classmates to share their own takeaways or understandings as a result of engaging in the work. If students are reading separate novels rather than a whole-class text, students can write their reviews and give particular attention to the themes or aspects of character development that emerged within the story. This particular means of analysis would then serve as a starting point, or thread, for group members to review their own works and see how the themes merge or diverge from one another. There are so many ways to utilize such platforms as we encourage students as both readers and writers of text.

Other Forms of Review

Aside from providing book reviews and analysis, or responding to written prompts for the purpose of recommending works and collaborating on texts together, students can flex their writing muscles through online purchase reviews, such as reviews on Amazon. As consumers, we want to be aware of what is available, appropriate, and enticing for our unique interests and needs. Teachers can encourage students to publish their reviews of a text through an online marketing program as a way of sharing their own takeaways from the story, while providing insight for those who might be considering the purchase or reading of a particular work.

Work with students to explicitly examine the components of an online review. What would they want to know about a product before making a purchase? What information would be important for them as consumers and potential product users? How can they effectively share this information within their own review? Then, have students examine reviews that have already been shared to the website. What do they notice about the selected reviews? What are the strengths in the writing? How do the reviewers convey their ideas and opinions of the product in terms of supporting facts or information? Once students are familiar with the structure and purpose of this writing, they can draft, revise, edit, and publish their own reviews for others to peruse and utilize within the selected website.

Professional Writing

As mentioned in the introduction of this chapter, technology has brought about new communication paradigms that have not only changed the way we define writing, but also the modes and forms of writing our students practice. One mode in particular, professional writing, has garnered a great deal of attention today. Professional writing forms include, but are not limited to, emails and resumes. In traditional classrooms, many of these forms of writing are often not practiced. Perhaps this is because standardized assessments do not assess a student's ability to craft professional writing. But given the importance of these literacy practices in the "real world," teachers should be addressing these forms of writing in their curriculum.

Emails

As virtual teachers, more than likely you have received "that email" from a student. You know, the email that reads as demanding in tone, containing words in all capital letters. And more than likely, your response to this email becomes similar in nature. But what if the intention of the author of the original email was the opposite? What if they did not realize that writing words in all capital letters has a connotation of yelling? More than likely, students have not been taught how to craft an email, yet it's the most practiced form of writing in the virtual classroom, not to mention in both the personal and professional realms as well.

Communication between teachers and students in the traditional classroom tends to be verbal in nature because of the face-to-face structure of the classroom. For virtual teachers who are separated from their students by both time and space, written communication often becomes the central form of communication. Because of this, virtual teachers have more opportunities to address this personal mode of writing than the traditional classroom teacher. Furthermore, for virtual teachers, teaching emails as a form of writing helps to not only prepare students for college or the workplace, but also prepares students to discuss author tone and voice in other forms of writing.

Beyond providing students with email framework and etiquette lessons, students need to practice this form of writing. One way teachers can engage students in this process is through real-time email communications with others, both inside and outside of their class. In class, teachers can create and utilize Google's Applied Digital Skills lessons to guide students through creating emails for different purposes. This site offers a guided lesson on how to craft, edit, and send an email for both professional and personal communications. Students begin by choosing an email scenario to practice. When students click on the scenario, they are greeted with a video that guides them through the necessary components of that particular type of email.

The students then have an opportunity to practice using another scenario. After two scenarios have been explored, students are then directed to view a video on how to edit and send an email. The final task in this application is reflection. Teachers can add to this lesson by creating several other email scenarios for students to work through. Students could then be asked to send these emails to their classmates, or to an assigned classroom partner. The partner, or classmates, can either respond to the email or assess the email in terms of etiquette and having the required components.

Beyond practicing emails with classmates, virtual teachers can expand this task by having students communicate with peers from around the world. Virtual teachers can connect with other virtual or classroom teachers and have students collaborate on projects or communicate about a common text being read. In a foreign language classroom, connecting to peers from other countries can provide students an opportunity to practice the language being learned.

There are several organizations that offer this opportunity for free. For example, ePals allows teachers to select specific criteria such as country, student age range, and content area. Empatico is another free online learning tool that allows teachers to match with another classroom across the world and collaborate on standards-based activities. Both platforms described also offer the opportunity for students to meet via video communications.

Resume

Writing for authentic purposes will motivate students, and there is nothing more authentic than writing something that students can use beyond the classroom. No matter if your students are planning to attend college and then enter the workforce, or move directly into the workforce, they will each be asked to submit a resume when applying for a job. This resume should spotlight their educational experiences, talents, skills, and achievements in a way that separates them from others. While this particular form of professional writing is one that is also not assessed on standardized tests, it is a skill that students will need to master in order to make themselves marketable in the professional world.

There are many ways a virtual teacher can approach resume writing in the online classroom. Asynchronously, students can be asked to work through a resume writing tutorial such as Resume Generator offered by ReadWriteThink. In this tutorial, students are guided through the elements of a resume and then create their own resume using the resume generator. Synchronously, virtual teachers can implement guided instruction on the elements of a resume and then have students review resumes as mentor texts.

As a whole class, the virtual teacher can walk students through an evaluation and critique of a resume using a few mentor texts. Ask students to look closely at the personal objective, goals, work experience, skills, and achievements presented in the resume. Ask students to consider the author's word choices and prompt them to offer additional words or descriptions they feel work better to "sell" this person. Virtual teachers could then create breakout rooms in which a team of students evaluates and critiques other mentor texts (resumes) and then return to the whole class to share their insights.

As an extension activity for either asynchronous or synchronous formats, the virtual teacher could share their experiences, achievements, skills, and talents with the students in person or through a recorded video, and ask the students to create a resume for them. This can be done individually or in teams. Students can share out the resume with the whole class, within a small group, or simply send the completed resume directly to the teacher.

Once students have had practice with evaluating and creating resumes, ask students to create their own resume. As they think through each of the components of the resume, they can work through several steps of the writing process as described in chapter 9. First ask students to brainstorm adjectives that describe their strengths and create a list of their skills, talents, and achievements.

Once students have generated these lists, guide them in choosing a professional position that they may one day wish to achieve. Keeping this career in mind, have students research the skills and traits that someone in this position must possess. Once they have completed their research, students should revisit their brainstorming list and either add to it or edit their word choices and write an objective. The final products can be shared as a whole class, in teams with their peers, or sent directly to the teacher.

Chapter Eleven

Conducting Writing Assessments in the Online Classroom

With virtual education maintaining such potential for isolation and disconnection, it is important to find ways of ensuring writing development. We want to translate what we know of formative and summative writing assessment into the virtual space in ways that not only provide insight into student growth, but also encourage student writing engagement on a consistent basis.

Assessing student writing is an important part of the writing process (Burke, 2009). When we evaluate student writing, an assessment serves "three main purposes: it provides guidance for revision of the current paper, it gives feedback students can use to improve their future performance, and it accounts for the grade you assign the paper" (Burke, 2009, p. 99). As such, in order "to obtain a complete picture of a student's writing skills, it is important that teachers take a balanced approach to assessment" (Hessler et al., 2009, p. 68). In other words, it requires teachers to assess both formatively and summatively.

As students work through the processes of writing, teachers must motivate, guide, and evaluate students' progression through each of the writing steps in order to ensure writing development is occurring and students are meeting the goals of the assigned writing. This chapter offers virtual teachers both formative and summative strategies through asynchronous and synchronous channels to accomplish this.

STRATEGIES FOR FORMATIVE WRITING ASSESSMENT

Formative writing assessment seeks to tap into what students are learning, and how they are developing as writers over time. Rather than assessing the final product, or demonstration of mastery within a particular writing domain, structure, or technique, formative writing assessment provides a checkpoint for student progress. As such, each of the following strategies works to provide teachers and students with greater insight into writing development within the virtual space, with less attention to grades or assessment scores.

Rubric Generators

Rubrics are tools that offer a means of evaluating student mastery of course content and skills in a systematic way. Teachers utilize rubrics for a variety of purposes at all levels and content areas. There are a variety of online rubric generators intended to assist teachers in crafting rubrics for their unique course assessments and projects. Students can also utilize such generators in crafting rubrics individually or as part of a whole class or small group to gain insight to and reflect on the key objectives or features of their final work.

When it comes to formative assessment, the focus is not as much on assessing for a final score or level of demonstrated mastery. Rather, rubrics can serve as starting points to give detailed, specific feedback on drafts of student work. Single-point rubrics are a wonderful resource for providing focused feedback regarding student progress (Dietz, 2000). As virtual teachers, you can identify a rubric generator that works for the purpose of your writing assignment and review. Then, craft a single-point rubric (see figure 11.1) to provide detailed feedback for your online learners. Notice how in this rubric, the focus lies on the feedback (areas of strength and areas of focused development), rather than on articulating a final grade. Such rubrics offer students opportunities to utilize the feedback, conference with the teacher regarding additional questions, and then continue to develop their writing ability and content based on suggestions and words of advice offered by the teacher or classmates.

Verbal Feedback

It's not always imperative that we provide feedback on our students' writing through text. In fact, students might find it beneficial to hear directly from their virtual teacher when it comes to their writing progress and course content or expectations. Not only can a voice put a stamp of reality and connection within the virtual context, but it can provide a sense of clarity at times of confusion or disengagement.

As students submit their writing for teacher review, or engage in a writing module, teachers can share questions and comments along the way as voice or video recordings. Using applications such as VoiceThread or simply using the recording device on the computer, teachers can provide students with this verbal feedback.

Areas of Development	Writing Criteria	Demonstration of Strength
Share areas the student can continue to develop with regard to the writing focus	Introduction	Share areas the student has demonstrated strength with regard to the writing focus
	Thesis	
	Identified Claims	
	Identified Support/ Evidence	

Figure 11.1. Single-point rubric example. *Created by the authors*

Sometimes, when listening to our verbal feedback, students may have questions along the way. One way to share feedback and elicit student input about the feedback being offered is through a formal writing conference. Virtual teachers can arrange a synchronous meeting via Zoom or Skype as a way to share and discuss feedback. Or a simple phone call to share feedback can suffice. Because you want students to use your feedback to further their writing development, using these strategies can allow virtual teachers to offer guidance to students about ways to address their feedback. Through this constructive response approach, you can positively impact students' writing development.

Conferencing

Writing conferences are a wonderful way to make space for students to create writing goals, reflect on their current abilities and areas of development as writers, and speak openly about their thoughts, experiences, and questions regarding writing and writing instruction. In chapter 1, we shared a variety of asynchronous and synchronous means of contacting and communicating with online learners. In addition to utilizing each of these strategies and tools to foster a relationship and connection, you can take advantage of these same approaches to engage in one-on-one writing conferencing throughout the course. As with the traditional classroom, strive to put the majority of the talking in the hands of the learner. What is it they want to understand or know more about? How do they view themselves as writers? How do they find that they are growing in their writing ability? What goal would they like to set for themselves in terms of their writing development, and what plan of action will they follow to achieve this goal?

Ideally, you want to find an effective means of synchronous conversation to really delve into the goals of the writing conference. But, if asynchronous appears to be your only means of contact, consider utilizing a tool such as Flipgrid to add a face and expression to the voice on the other end of the computer screen. Encourage two-way communication as you engage in initial and ongoing writing conferencing with each of your virtual learners. As a means of formative assessment, the key is ongoing conferencing throughout the learning and writing process. Keep track of student reflection and development. Help them maintain their goals and reflect on how they are continuing to develop as writers throughout the duration of the online course.

Peer Feedback

Just as teacher-to-student conferencing is beneficial to setting personalized writing goals, students can benefit from communication and feedback from their classmates. Collaborative learning has the benefit of engaging students in learning that extends beyond their singular perspective or understanding. As students engage in the act of writing, they can share their brainstorming and work with peers, discuss their ideas, questions, and concerns together, and utilize one another's assets in furthering their own development.

In chapter 9, we shared strategies for engaging students in collaborative learning throughout the writing process. In terms of assessment, students can continue to collaborate and learn from one another about developing and finalizing their writing. Peer feedback can give students ideas regarding the strengths and areas of need within their creative, expository, or argumentative writing pieces. It also has the potential to enhance student engagement, as writers are able to connect with peers, read the work their peers are producing in response to the course material, and step out of potential isolation. In addition, teachers can identify the ways in which students are critically examining and evaluating one another's work. What do students gravitate toward when providing peer feedback? What appears to be missing or lost in the feedback process? How might you, as virtual teachers, continue to lead students in effective peer review and feedback?

It can be helpful to explicitly teach students effective review procedures and processes. You might also generate an online rubric or graphic organizer for students to utilize as they read and respond to one another's work. Ensure students are aware of the objective of the peer review process, what is expected of their feedback, and how such feedback aims to assist their classmates in furthering their writing ability. If working within an asynchronous platform, provide timelines so that students who engage in the course at different hours on different days are more apt to meet designated deadlines for the benefit of their peers. You can also consider utilizing a variety of online mediums (shared files, apps, etc.) for students to review and provide feedback. Just because students are unable to meet face to face, it does not mean they are limited in their ability to work together in assessing and developing their work. Take advantage of the many collaborative learning platforms noted throughout this book to engage students in peer-to-peer correspondence.

Student Self-Assessment and Reflection

Finally, we understand the advantages of encouraging student meta-cognition through self-reflection and assessment. While it is advantageous for teachers and peers to provide formative feedback to students, it is also important to provide opportunities for virtual learners to review their own development and reflect on this development over time. The online platform provides a wonderful opportunity for students to maintain an ongoing record of their development as writers over time. Whether they maintain an online notebook using a platform such as Google Docs, a series of personal videos recorded within an application such as Flipgrid, or an audio thread documented within an application such as VoiceThread, students can log what they are learning, how they are building on prior skills, and aspects of their writing they would like to continue to develop.

Students can also engage in self-assessment of particular works using a single-point rubric all their own. Just as teachers can take advantage of single-point rubrics as a means of providing detailed feedback on a particular writing sample, students can also complete a single-point rubric to critically examine particular aspects of their own work. Encourage students to be honest in assessing work, but to avoid overstating their strengths or ruminating on their needs. You want students to maintain a growth mindset—attention to their potential for growth—throughout the self-assessment process, rather than dwell on what they might identify as personal flaws or shortcomings. Virtual teachers can assist students in reaching this goal as they review student self-assessments and reflections and continue to encourage students through response videos, audio replies, or document comments.

STRATEGIES FOR SUMMATIVE WRITING ASSESSMENT

Online Portfolio of Student Writing

Writing portfolios hold great promise as a means of summative writing assessment. Students select the work they feel represents their "best work," and utilize the portfolio as a means of demonstrating their knowledge and abilities as authors. Thanks to the virtual space, writing portfolios now extend beyond the confines of a manila folder or binder. Students can take advantage of online databases and applications to maintain a digital portfolio. Teachers can create online folders for students to update within a learning management system, such as Google Classroom or Blackboard. Such files can provide privacy for student work, as well as an opportunity for teachers to provide feedback and grading within the denoted system. Or, students can utilize a more public domain to house the compilation of their final work. Websites such as Wix, Squarespace, and Weebly offer digital space for students to maintain their writing portfolios. Just be sure to review the cost, accessibility, and feasibility of each site when selecting one that works for you and your students.

Published Writing

In chapter 10, we shared suggestions for publishing student writing as a means of finalizing the writing process. In navigating summative assessment, teachers can reference published works to gauge student mastery and writing ability. Much like the digital portfolio, published work represents the student's final piece and evidence of student writing development and learning over the course of the writing process.

Rubrics as Summative Assessment

Finally, teachers can utilize rubrics as a means of summative assessment. Rubrics provide space for teachers to identify how they might assess assorted aspects of student writing for proficiency or mastery. In addition, quality rubrics offer students insight into the objectives of their work, as well as understanding of what is required or expected of their final text. Rubric generators such as RubiStar, Rubric Maker, and Quick Rubric provide an easy way to generate an original rubric for the purpose of your unique course assessment.

References

Allen, J. (2000). *Yellow brick roads: Shared and guided paths to independent reading 4–12.* Stenhouse Publishers.

Alvermann, D. E. (2002). Effective literacy instruction for adolescents. *Journal of Literacy Research, 34*(2), 189–208.

Anderson, R. C. (1994). Role of the reader's schema in comprehension, learning, and memory. In R. B. Ruddell, M. R. Ruddell, & H. Singer (Eds.), *Theoretical models and processes of reading* (pp. 469–482). International Reading Association.

Bloome, D. (2001). Building literacy and the classroom community. *Theory into Practice, 15*(2), 71–76.

Burke, J. (2009). *Content area writing.* Scholastic Teaching Resources.

Burke, J. (2010). *What's the big idea?: Question-driven units to motivate reading, writing, and thinking.* Heinemann.

Christenbury, L. (2006). *Making the journey.* Heinemann.

Costa, A. L., & Kallick, B. (2000). Getting into the habit of reflection. *Educational Leadership, 57*(7), 60–62.

Daniels, H. (2002). *Literature circles voice and choice in book clubs and reading groups* (2nd ed.). Stenhouse.

Dietz, M. (2000). Single point rubric idea presented at INTASC Academy, July 12–21, Alverno College, Milwaukee, WI.

Dunn, K. E., & Mulvenon, S. W. (2009). A critical review of research on formative assessments: The limited scientific evidence of the impact of formative assessments in education. *Practical Assessment, Research & Evaluation, 14*(7), 1–11.

Edwards-Groves, C. J. (2011). The multimodal writing process: Changing practices in contemporary classrooms. *Language and Education, 25*(1), 49–64.

Eisenbach, B., Greathouse, P., and Kirk, M. (2018). Creating a community of care in the middle level virtual classroom. In B. Eisenbach & P. Greathouse (Eds.), *The online classroom: Resources for effective middle level virtual education* (pp. 121–136). Information Age Publishing.

Fisher, D., & Frey, N. (2016). *Improving adolescent literacy: Content area reading strategies at work.* Pearson.

Fredricks, J. A., Blumenfeld, P. C., & Paris, A. H. (2004). School engagement: Potential of the concept, state of evidence. *Review of Educational Research, 74*, 59–109.

Fulwiler, T. (1980). Journals across the disciplines. *English Journal, 69*(9), 14–19.

Gallagher, K. (2006). *Teaching adolescent writers.* Stenhouse.

Grant, A., Hutchinson, K., Hornsby, D., & Brooke, S. (2008). Creative pedagogies: "Art-Full" reading and writing. *English Teaching: Practice and Critique, 7*(1), 57–72.

Gunter, G., & Kenny, R. (2008). Digital booktalk: Digital media for reluctant readers. *Contemporary Issues in Technology & Teacher Education, 8*(1), 84–99.

Guthrie, J. T., & Wigfield, A. (2000). Engagement and motivation in reading. In M. L. Kamil, P. B. Mosenthal, P. D. Pearson, & R. Barr (Eds.), *Handbook of reading research, volume 3* (pp. 403–422). Lawrence Erlbaum Associates.

Hall, L. A. (2012). The role of reading identities and reading abilities in students' discussions about texts and comprehension strategies. *Journal of Literacy Research, 44*(4), 239–272.

Harmon, J. M., Hedrick, W. B., & Fox, E. A. (2000). A content analysis of vocabulary instruction in social studies textbooks for grades 4–8. *Elementary School Journal, 100*(3), 253–271.

Harrington, S., Rickly, R., & Day, M. (Eds.). (2000). *The online writing classroom*. Hampton Press, Inc.

Hessler, T., Konrad, M., & Alber-Morgan, S. (2009). Assess student writing. *Intervention in School and Clinic, 45*(1), 68–71.

Hinton, S. E. (1967/2006). *The outsiders*. Speak.

Hobson, T. D., & Puruhito, K. K. (2018). Going the distance: Online course performance and motivation of distance-learning students. *Online Learning, 22*(4), 129–140.

Hogan, T. (1980). Students' interest in writing activities. *Research in the Teaching of English, 14*(2), 119–126.

Holdren, T. (2012). Using art to assess reading comprehension and critical thinking in adolescents. *Journal of Adolescent and Adult Literacy, 55*(8), 692–703.

Houge, T. T., Peyton, D., Geier, C., & Petrie, B. (2007). Adolescent literacy tutoring: Face-to-face and via webcam technology. *Reading Psychology, 28*(3), 283–300.

Ivanic, R. (1998). *Writing and identity: The discoursal construction of identity in academic writing*. John Benjamins.

Jones, R. C. (2012, August 26). Strategies for reading comprehension: Questioning the author. *Reading Quest*. http://www.readingquest.org/strat/qta.html

Kucer, S. B. (2009). *Dimensions of literacy: A conceptual base for teaching reading and writing in school settings*. Routledge.

Lake, P. K., Hass, B. K., & Matthews, M. (2014). Fit to care: An action research study exploring the use of Communication Theory to strengthen caring relationships between teachers and students. *International Journal for Human Caring, 18*(3), 15–25.

Livingston, C. (2005). Journals of discovery: Incorporating art and creative writing into science journals leads to meaningful reflections on learning for both students and teachers. *Science and Children, 43*(3), 52–55.

Marzano, R. J., Pickering, D., & Pollock, J. E. (2001). *Classroom instruction that works: Research-based strategies for increasing student achievement*. Association for Supervision and Curriculum Development.

McElhone, D. (2014). *Text talk: Engaging readers in purposeful discussion*. International Reading Association. http://www.literacyworldwide.org/docs/default-source/member-benefits/e-ssentials/ila-e-ssentials-8045.pdf

McKeown, M., Hamilton, R., Kucan, L., & Beck. I. (1997). *Questioning the author: An approach for enhancing student engagement with text*. International Literacy Association.

Mercer, N., & Littleton, K. (2007). *Dialogue and the development of children's thinking*. Routledge.

Miller, S., & Hopper, P. (2010). Supporting reading goals through visual arts. *Reading Improvement, 47*(1), 3–6.

Moje, E. B., Young, J. P., Readence, J. E., & Moore, D. W. (2000). Commentary: Reinventing adolescent literacy for new times: Perennial and millennial issues. *Journal of Adolescent & Adult Literacy, 43*(5), 400–410.

Nichols, M. (2008). *Talking about text: Guiding students to increase comprehension through purposeful talk*. Shell Education.

Nwokoreze, U. (1990). Note-taking. *English Teaching Forum, 33*(2), 39–40.

Ogle, D. M. (1986). K-W-L: A teaching model that develops active reading of expository text. *The Reading Teacher, 39*(6), 564–570.

Owusu-Ansah, A., & Kyei-Blankson, L. (2016). Going back to the basics: Demonstrating care, connectedness, and a pedagogy of relationship in education. *World Journal of Education, 6*(3), 1–9.

Park, J. (2012). A different kind of reading instruction: Using visualizing to bridge reading comprehension and critical literacy. *Journal of Adolescent & Adult Literacy, 55*(7), 629–640.

Potts, J. A. (2019). Profoundly gifted students' perceptions of virtual classrooms. *Gifted Child Quarterly, 63*(1), 58–80.

Rief, L. (1991). *Seeking diversity: Language arts with adolescents.* Heinemann.

Romiszowski, A. J., & Mason, R. (2004). Computer-mediated communication. In D. H. Jonassen (Ed.), *Handbook of research for educational communications and technology* (pp. 397–431). Lawrence Erlbaum Associates.

Rosenblatt, L. M. (1978). *The reader, the text, the poem: The transactional theory of the literary work* (revised paperback edition). Southern Illinois University Press.

Rovai, A. P. (2003). In search of higher persistence rates in distance education online programs. *The Internet and Higher Education, 6*(1), 1–16.

Ryan, R. M., & Deci, E. L. (2000). Intrinsic and extrinsic motivations: Classic definitions and new directions. *Contemporary Educational Psychology, 25*(1), 54–67.

Seban, D., & Tavsanlı, Ö. F. (2015). Children's sense of being a writer: Identity construction in second grade writers workshop. *International Electronic Journal of Elementary Education, 7*(2), 217– 234.

Simon, C. A. (2015). *Strategy guides: Questioning the author (QtA).* ReadWriteThink. http://www.readwritethink.org/professional-development/strategy-guides/question-author-30761.html?main-tab=1#main-tabs

Taboada, A., & Guthrie, J. T. (2004). Growth of cognitive strategies for reading comprehension. In J. T. Guthrie, A. Wigfield, & K. C. Perencevich (Eds.), *Motivating reading comprehension: Concept-oriented reading instruction* (pp. 273–306). Erlbaum.

Thomas, A. (2017). *The hate u give.* Balzer + Bray.

Thomas, P. L., Goering, C. Z., & Cridland-Hughes, S. (2015). Speaking truth to power: Caring critical literacy: The most radical pedagogy you can offer students. *English Journal, 105*(2), 129–132.

Vanslambrouck, S., Zhu, C., Lombaerts, K., Philipsen, B., & Tondeur, J. (2017). Students' motivation and subjective task value of participating in online and blended learning environments. *The Internet and Higher Education, 36*, 33–40.

Vasquez, V., & Felderman, C. (2012). *Technology and critical literacy in early childhood.* Routledge.

White, B. (2003). Caring and the teaching of English. *Research in the Teaching of English, 37*(3), 295–328.

About the Authors

Brooke Eisenbach, PhD, is associate professor of middle and secondary education at Lesley University. She is a former middle school English and Young Adult Literature teacher and taught students ages twelve to nineteen within an English I virtual school course. She has been published in journals such as *English Journal* and *Educational Leadership* and is the coeditor of *The Online Classroom: Resources for Effective Middle Level Virtual Education—The Handbook of Resources in Middle Level Education* (2018). She is an active member of the National Council of Teachers of English (NCTE) Standing Committee Against Censorship and Middle Level Steering Committee. She has won several awards, including the Florida Council of Teachers of English Teacher of the Year Award and the NCTE Outstanding Middle Level Educator in the English Language Arts Award.

Paula Greathouse, PhD, is associate professor of secondary English education at Tennessee Tech University. She is a former secondary ELA and Reading teacher and was the cocreator and teacher of the dropout prevention online English program in her former school district. She has been published in journals such as *Educational Action Research*, *The Clearing House*, and *English Journal* and is the coeditor of *The Online Classroom: Resources for Effective Middle Level Virtual Education—The Handbook of Resources in Middle Level Education* (2018). She is an active member of the NCTE, serving as an elected member of the English Language Arts Teacher Education Nominating Committee and current chair of the Standing Committee Against Censorship. She has received several teaching awards, including the NCTE Teacher of Excellence Award.

www.ingramcontent.com/pod-product-compliance
Lightning Source LLC
Chambersburg PA
CBHW030146240426
43672CB00005B/290